CAMBRIDGE LIBRARY COLLECTION

Books of enduring scholarly value

Literary Studies

This series provides a high-quality selection of early printings of literary works, textual editions, anthologies and literary criticism which are of lasting scholarly interest. Ranging from Old English to Shakespeare to early twentieth-century work from around the world, these books offer a valuable resource for scholars in reception history, textual editing, and literary studies.

Shakespeare's Hand in the Play of *Sir Thomas More*

First published in 1923, this book consists of a series of papers written by Pollard, W.W. Greg, E. Maunde Thompson, J. Dover Wilson, and R.W. Chambers, all advocates of the then newly-established New Bibliography. The book was assembled with the intention of strengthening the argument that three pages of *Sir Thomas More* in the Harleian Manuscript at the British Museum were written in Shakespeare's own hand. The well-established scholars examine the case from several different angles, considering the handwriting in comparison to the known versions of Shakespeare's signature, the bibliographical links between these three pages and the 'good' quartos, and the content of the pages in relation to political ideas expressed elsewhere in Shakespeare. The volume also includes plates of Shakespeare's signatures, analysis of individual letter shapes and parts of the manuscript, and a special transcript of the pages in question.

Cambridge University Press has long been a pioneer in the reissuing of out-of-print titles from its own backlist, producing digital reprints of books that are still sought after by scholars and students but could not be reprinted economically using traditional technology. The Cambridge Library Collection extends this activity to a wider range of books which are still of importance to researchers and professionals, either for the source material they contain, or as landmarks in the history of their academic discipline.

Drawing from the world-renowned collections in the Cambridge University Library, and guided by the advice of experts in each subject area, Cambridge University Press is using state-of-the-art scanning machines in its own Printing House to capture the content of each book selected for inclusion. The files are processed to give a consistently clear, crisp image, and the books finished to the high quality standard for which the Press is recognised around the world. The latest print-on-demand technology ensures that the books will remain available indefinitely, and that orders for single or multiple copies can quickly be supplied.

The Cambridge Library Collection will bring back to life books of enduring scholarly value (including out-of-copyright works originally issued by other publishers) across a wide range of disciplines in the humanities and social sciences and in science and technology.

Shakespeare's Hand in the Play of *Sir Thomas More*

EDITED BY W.W. GREG

CAMBRIDGE
UNIVERSITY PRESS

CAMBRIDGE UNIVERSITY PRESS

Cambridge, New York, Melbourne, Madrid, Cape Town, Singapore,
São Paolo, Delhi, Dubai, Tokyo

Published in the United States of America by Cambridge University Press, New York

www.cambridge.org
Information on this title: www.cambridge.org/9781108015356

© in this compilation Cambridge University Press 2010

This edition first published 1967
This digitally printed version 2010

ISBN 978-1-108-01535-6 Paperback

SHAKESPEARE'S HAND IN
The PLAY *of* Sir THOMAS MORE

PAPERS by ALFRED W. POLLARD
W. W. GREG E. MAUNDE THOMPSON
J. DOVER WILSON & R. W. CHAMBERS

with the text of the Ill May Day Scenes
edited by W. W. Greg

CAMBRIDGE
AT THE UNIVERSITY PRESS
1923

REPRINTED
1967

Published by the Syndics of the
Cambridge University Press
Bentley House, 200 Euston Road, London, N.W. 1
American Branch: 32 East 57th Street,
New York, N.Y. 10022

PUBLISHER'S NOTE

Cambridge University Press Library Editions are reissues
of out-of-print standard works from the Cambridge
catalogue. The texts are unrevised and, apart from minor
corrections, reproduce the latest published edition.

First published 1923
Reprinted 1967

First printed in Great Britain
at the University Printing House, Cambridge
Reprinted in the United States of America
Library of Congress Catalogue Card Number: 24-13051

PREFACE

THE object of this book is to strengthen the evidence of the existence (in the Harleian MS. 7368 at the British Museum) of three pages written by Shakespeare in his own hand as part of the play of *Sir Thomas More*. The contributors have tried not to be over-eager in pressing their contention, or to claim more than they can make good. They would not have their readers less critical than they have tried to be themselves, and are aware that from one quarter at least searching criticism is to be expected, since if Shakespeare wrote these three pages the discrepant theories which unite in regarding the "Stratford man" as a mere mask concealing the activity of some noble lord (a 17th Earl of Oxford, a 6th Earl of Derby, or a Viscount St Albans) come crashing to the ground. It is here contended that the writing of the three pages is compatible with a development into the hand seen in Shakespeare's considerably later extant signatures and explains misprints in his text; that the spelling of the three pages can all be paralleled from the text of the best editions of single plays printed in Shakespeare's life, and that the temper and even the phrasing of the three pages in the two crucial points involved, the attitude to authority and the attitude to the crowd, agree with and render more intelligible passages in much later plays. In the Introduction it is shown that the most likely date at which the three pages were written is one which easily admits of their composition by Shakespeare for the company for which he habitually wrote. All these contentions may be mistaken; but the Editor may at least claim for his contributors that they have earned a right to their opinions and that their conclusions cannot lightly be dismissed. While there has been some friendly interchange of criticism each contributor must be understood as taking responsibility only for his own paper.

Grateful acknowledgement is offered to the Delegates of the Clarendon Press for their kindness in allowing use to be made of the facsimiles of the six signatures in Sir E. Maunde Thompson's book on *Shakespeare's Handwriting* published by them in 1916.

A. W. POLLARD.

June 1923

CONTENTS

PLATES

I. INTRODUCTION

By Alfred W. Pollard

I

THE writers of the successive chapters of this book are interested in the old play of *Sir Thomas More* mainly because, on various grounds and with varying degrees of confidence, they believe that part of a scene, represented by three pages of the extant manuscript, was composed and written with his own hand by Shakespeare. Yet the play has some interest in its own right and the section in which the three pages occur makes a very popular appeal. Although in the end the hero goes (manfully and merrily) to an unjust death with the full sympathy of the reader, or hypothetical spectator, the play is not a tragedy, hardly even a chronicle history. It is made up of three groups of scenes, each group being fairly homogeneous and the scenes composing it with one exception consecutive. The first group (scenes i and iii–vii) describes from beginning to end the anti-alien riots on the 'ill May-day' of 1517, the quelling of which is, with very scant historical justification, attributed to More's pacifying oratory, and represented as promptly rewarded by knighthood (which was conferred on him in 1521), membership of the Privy Council (conferred in 1518) and Lord Chancellorship (conferred in 1529). Of the scenes of the second group (ii, viii, ix) the earliest shows More, while one of the city Sheriffs (he was really a permanent under-Sheriff), saving a thief from the gallows as a reward for his help in a practical joke on a pompous city justice; in the later scenes we see him changing clothes with his steward in order to trick his friend Erasmus (who had known him since 1497), giving an offensively long-haired servitor his choice between prison and the barber (a story told in Foxe's *Book of Martyrs* of Thomas Cromwell and here, rather unhappily, transferred to More) and stepping in to supply by improvisation the place of a missing actor in an interlude performed in his own house for the entertainment of the Lord Mayor and Mayoress. Finally, the scenes of the third group (scenes x–xvii) exhibit More's refusal to sign certain mysterious 'articles' presented to him in the King's name, his resignation of the Chancellorship, and the successive steps by which his seclusion in his own house at Chelsea was followed by his arrest as a traitor, despatch to the Tower, condemnation and execution.

The four episodes of the second group of scenes are not very successful. The trick played on the pompous justice is well told up to almost the end and then goes to pieces; the trick on Erasmus is badly muddled; the treatment of the long-haired servitor seems to have aroused some doubts, as there are variant endings to it; the improvisation is the best of the four, but rather a slight matter to make so much of. Even if much more perfectly set forth these stories would form a very inadequate link between the picture of More's (much accelerated) rise to power and his (equally accelerated) fall, condemnation and death.

The last group of scenes show touches of dignity, humour and pathos; but the writers do not rise to the height of their argument, partly because they had not

the courage explicitly to state it. More is shown refusing to sign the articles exhibited to him by the
King's command, but the contents of the articles are
carefully left unexplained. Elizabeth retained the
ecclesiastical supremacy which More died rather than
approve, and blind as these playwrights were to the
difficulties in their path they had at least the wit to
see what must inevitably happen if they let him argue
his case.

In the first group of scenes there is no such hesitation. The writers explain quite clearly what the 'ill
May-day' riots were about, and they are so full of
their subject that now and again they almost forget
their hero. In the two other groups of scenes More
is always in our minds. Even when Bishop Fisher
crosses the stage on the way to the Tower we think
not of him, but of More and the penalty he too will
have to pay. The anti-alien scenes are written for
their own sake; they come very near indeed to being
a complete play in themselves, a play in which More
appears as Athene might in some Greek tragedy, full
of reasonableness and persuasive wisdom, surpassing
the hero and heroine and yet not displacing them in
our affections. The hero and heroine are Lincoln and
Doll Williamson; and our *deus ex machina*, Sheriff
More, suffers somewhat in our esteem because the
hard facts of history made it impossible for him to be
represented as saving Lincoln from the gallows as (in
the play) he was deeply pledged to do. The effect of
this miniature play is weakened by the interposition
of the Sessions scene with its presentation (at once
lengthy and a little ragged) of the joke More plays on
the city justice, and again by the heaviness of the two
groups of scenes by which it is followed. It is a

pleasure to print the miniature play for the first time without these encumbrances. It is a pity that the main purpose of our book forbids us to edit it specifically for the enjoyment of modern readers, as it deserves.

Of course the miniature anti-alien play was doomed from the start to be censored out of existence. It may be doubted whether a modern counterpart of it would easily be passed for performance. The manuscript shows us that a scene in which apprentices wound Sir John Munday (Anthony no doubt introduced this out of family pride) was cut out, as dramatically superfluous and likely to cause trouble, and the climax of the riot was re-written, no doubt also to conciliate the censor. At first the censor himself, Edmund Tilney, seems to have thought that something might be done by botching. He marks individual passages for omission, and substitutes 'Lombards' for 'Frenchmen' or 'strangers,' as there were few Lombards in London at the time the play was written, whereas Huguenots from France and refugees from Spanish persecution in the Low Countries were many, and the Londoners had little love for them. But when he had got to the end of the 'ill May-day' scenes he obviously saw that half measures would be useless, so he went back to the beginning of the play and wrote in the margin the drastic order

Leaue out yᵉ insurrection wholy & yᵉ cause theroff & begin wᵗ Sʳ Tho: More att yᵉ mayors sessions wᵗ a reportt afterwards off his good seruic don being Shriue off London vppon a mutiny agaynst yᵉ Lumbards. Only by a shortt reportt & nott otherwise att your own perrilles. E. Tyllney.

The use of the name of an actor Goodal in the margin of leaf 13* recto for the part of a Messenger, and an attempt (see Dr Greg's note) to reduce the number of actors needed to play scene vi, proves that the players had been sufficiently hopeful of securing a licence to 'cast' the play for performance. But this drastic order must have convinced them that the play was hopeless, and I agree with Dr Greg that the re-writing of the climax of the riot in the three pages with which we are specially concerned should be looked on as an anticipatory attempt to placate Tilney, rather than a (quite inadequate) effort to comply with his order. In the first of these three pages the spectator is no longer invited to sympathize with the objects of the crowd, but to laugh at it amiably and note its foibles. In the speech which follows, in which More persuades the rioters to submit, he puts the case for obedience to the royal authority at its very highest, opposition to the King being represented as opposition to God Himself. The players forgot that there might be subjects which Authority would not allow to be presented on the stage, however judiciously they were handled, and that the rising of a London mob against the foreigners whom it was the policy of Authority to welcome might be one of them. But that the sub-stitution of the three pages of the manuscript in which the mob is ridiculed and obedience to the sovereign exalted for the original scene which they displace was due to a desire to propitiate Authority seems certain.

The belief which underlies this book is that in anticipation of trouble with the censor the players had turned to an 'absolute Johannes factotum' who had previously had no part in the play, and that it is thus no accident that in these three pages we find the attitude to mobs, the attitude to the crown, and the deep humanity, which are recurrent features in the work of William Shakespeare.

II[1]

The play of *Sir Thomas More* was first printed in 1844 in an edition prepared for the *Shakespeare Society* by the Rev. Alexander Dyce, who bestowed much care on the task of transcribing the difficult manuscript (Harl. 7368 at the British Museum) in which alone it has come down to us, but contented himself with a single page preface and some extracts from Halle's chronicle and a ballad on the Evil Mayday of 1517 by way of introduction.

Twenty-seven years after the appearance of Dyce's edition Richard Simpson (a liberal Roman Catholic theologian who towards the end of his life interested himself greatly in Shakespeare) in an article in *Notes and Queries* for July 1, 1871 (4th series, Vol. VIII), entitled 'Are there any extant MSS. in Shakespeare's Handwriting?' claimed two sections of our play as in Shakespeare's autograph. Simpson based this claim mainly on the literary evidence, the 'Shakespearian flavour' of these sections, but also on the character of the handwriting, asserting that 'the way in which the letters are formed is absolutely the same as the way in which they are formed in the signatures of Shakespeare.' On September 21 of the following year James Spedding took up Simpson's argument, again in *Notes and Queries*, with a keen sense of its importance. He suggested that the relevant pages of the manuscript should be printed in facsimile to facilitate their study, and at the same time reduced those which

[1] Some use has here been made, by permission, of an article contributed to *The Times*, Literary Supplement, 24 April, 1919.

he thought could be assigned to Shakespeare to three, on which is written the greater part of a scene describing the pacification by More of the anti-alien riot of 1517. As to these he wrote, very justly:

If there is in the British Museum an entire dramatic scene filling three pages of fifty lines each, composed by Shakespeare when he was about twenty-five years old[1], and *written out with his own hand*, it is a 'new fact' of much more value than all the new facts put together which have caused so much hot controversy of late years. As a curiosity it would command a high price; but it is better than a curiosity. To know what kind of hand Shakespeare wrote would often help to discover what words he wrote.

For a third of a century the seed sown by Simpson and watered by Spedding bore fruit only in occasional references, but in 1908 the play was included in the *Shakespearian Apocrypha* published by the Oxford University Press under the editorship of Mr C. F. Tucker-Brooke and in 1910 by the enterprise of the late Mr J. S. Farmer not merely the 'relevant pages,' for which Spedding had asked, but the entire manuscript was published in facsimile.

In 1911 a great step forward was taken by the production for the Malone Society by Dr W. W. Greg of an edition of the play which must always rank among the best examples of English literary and palæographical scholarship. In this the present state of the manuscript was carefully described and it was divided palæographically into thirteen leaves in a main hand (called S), seven leaves of Additions in five different hands (called A–E) and some notes by a censor, easily identified with Edmund Tilney, Master

---

[1] Dyce had dated the play 'about 1590 or perhaps a little earlier.'

of the Revels, one of whose duties it was to grant or withhold licences for the public performance of plays. In Dr Greg's classification the three pages assigned to Shakespeare by Simpson, as amended by Spedding, are in hand D. As to these Dr Greg wrote:

These hasty pages of D's have individual qualities which mark them off sharply from the rest of the play. There is wit in the humours of the crowd, there is something like passion in More's oratory. So striking indeed are these qualities that more than one critic has persuaded himself that the lines in question can have come from no pen but Shakespeare's. The possibility acquires additional interest from the fact that the passage is undoubtedly autograph. Here possibly are three pages in the hand that so many have desired to see. The question is one of stylistic evidence, and each reader will have to judge for himself. I do not feel called upon to pronounce: but I will say this much, that it seems to me an eminently reasonable view that would assign this passage to the writer who, as I believe, foisted certain of the Jack Cade scenes into the second part of *Henry VI*.

By a comparison with MS. Addit. 30262 fol. 66^b at the British Museum and with Henslowe's Diary fols. 101 and 114, at Dulwich College, Dr Greg had identified the hand of one of the Additions to the play (that which he calls E) as Thomas Dekker's. In 1912, again by the enterprise of Mr Farmer, the publication of a facsimile of Munday's play *John a Kent and John a Cumber*, then in possession of Lord Mostyn, showed (as was promptly pointed out by Dr Greg) that this manuscript is autograph and that the writing is that of the bulk of *Sir Thomas More*, that of the hand S to which we owe the thirteen original leaves. Thus we now know that these thirteen leaves were written by Anthony Munday, though the occurrence of the curious mistake 'fashis,' for fashiō, i.e. fashion, in line †1847 (Greg's numeration), which no author could make in transcribing his own manuscript, proves that for some of these thirteen leaves he was only a copyist.

The manuscripts of *John a Kent* and *Sir Thomas More* are connected not only by the first being wholly and the second in part in Munday's writing, but also by both being cased in leaves from the same fifteenth century Breviary or Legenda, *John a Kent* having also a patch from a thirteenth century copy of the *Compilatio prima* of Canon Law by Bernard of Pavia. Each, moreover, is inscribed on the front wrapper with its title (the word 'booke' being used in each case: *The Booke of John a Kent and John a Cumber* and *The Booke of Sir Thomas Moore*), in large engrossing characters. The two plays must thus have been in the same hands at the same time, and they must also have continued probably for some years in the same ownership, as both have suffered in the same way from damp which has rotted the outer margins of the paper leaves of both manuscripts in like manner.

The *More* manuscript is undated; that of *John a Kent* below Munday's signature at the end of the play bears a mutilated date '...Decembris 1596,' in a fine Italian hand differing from Munday's writing of the same class and in a different ink. The mutilation is unlucky, as on the probable supposition that the inscription was put midway in the breadth of the page there is room for more than the word 'die' and a number (which must have preceded 'Decembris'), and if another word preceded the day of the month, this might have revealed the meaning of the date which at present is mysterious. The only point tolerably certain is that it cannot be the date at which Munday completed and signed the play. Had it been this he would surely have written it with his own hand, it would have come more to the right on the page in immediate connection with his signature and would hardly have been in Latin. Latin, if we may generalize from other notes in books, would be appropriate to a date of purchase, and if so, the date would presumably be either that at which it was acquired by the company of players by whom it was acted, or that at which some private purchaser recorded his purchase of it from the company. The refinement of the hand and the use of Latin both support the latter alternative, and if Fleay's identification of *John a Kent* with *The Wise Man of Westchester* acted by the Admiral's men in and after the autumn of 1594 is not now to be rejected this view must certainly be preferred.

Three or four years after the publication of the facsimile of Munday's *John a Kent*, which led to the identification of the main hand of *Sir Thomas More* as his, Sir Edward Maunde Thompson in contributing a chapter on 'Handwriting' to the book on *Shakespeare's England*,' with which the delegates of Oxford University Press in 1916 were to celebrate the tercentenary of Shakespeare's death, passed in review all the various signatures, etc. which had at any time been attributed to Shakespeare. He condemned all the signatures[1] save those respectively attached to

[1] In a subsequent paper contributed to *The Library* (3rd Series, July, 1917, Vol. VIII) Sir Edward gave *in extenso* his reasons for regarding as forged the signature in the copy of Florio's translation of the *Essays* of Montaigne, acquired by the British Museum at the instance of Sir Frederick Madden, and also that on the Bodleian Ovid.

Shakespeare's deposition (11 May 1612) in the suit of Stephen Bellott *v.* Christopher Montjoy, to the conveyance of the house in Blackfriars bought by him (10 March 1613) and the mortgage deed of the same (11 March 1613) and the three to his Will (25 March 1616). When, however, he came to the three pages in the More manuscript he recognized in the hand D of the Additions 'certain features' which he had already noted in Shakespeare's signatures. After an exhaustive study of the manuscript he became convinced that here he was in truth confronted with a holograph literary manuscript of our greatest English poet. Late in 1916 he published his conclusions and the evidence on which they were based in a monograph entitled *Shakespeare's Handwriting* (Oxford, at the Clarendon Press), with full facsimiles of the three pages and an independent transliteration of them, differing in a few minute points from that in Dr Greg's edition.

Sir E. M. Thompson's arguments were respectfully received and there was a general acknowledgment by reviewers of the exceptional skill with which the scanty evidence was marshalled and analysed. But even if his monograph had appeared at some quieter time than the very middle of the great war, it would probably have met with a somewhat inert reception, as the number of trained palæographers is but small, and few of this small number have made any special study of the handwriting of Shakespeare's day. Thoroughly to test the conclusions reached requires not only some preliminary knowledge, but much patient investigation and a gift of palæographic vision of a very unusual kind.

III

The task with which anyone is confronted who tries to draw conclusions as to the authorship of the three pages of the play of *Sir Thomas More* by comparing the hand in which they are written with the hand of the six signatures is not the comparatively easy one of establishing or disproving the identity of two literary hands of approximately the same date. It is not even the much harder task of establishing identity between a literary hand and contemporary signatures. It is the almost impossibly difficult enterprise of stating, to himself and others, the ground for his own belief that the hand which wrote the three pages probably, as will be shown, late in 1593 or early in 1594, possibly a year later, would, or would not, naturally develop in the course of the next eighteen to twenty years in such a way as to produce the signature to the deposition of 1612, the two signatures to the deeds of 1613 and the three signatures to the will of 1616, all six of them written under the eyes of lawyers, and all six of them, we may surely guess, in moods as unlike those of dramatic composition as can well be conceived. The problem is thus first to visualize how a handwriting after a lapse of some twenty years and in totally different circumstances will show the natural effects of these and yet preserve its identity, and secondly, to make the process thus visualized intelligible to others not specially equipped to deal with it.

In comparing contemporary specimens of handwriting in each of which alternative forms are used for the same letter, if we are to establish identity we must show not merely that both the variants are present in each of the specimens, or groups of specimens, but that they are present in approximately the same proportions. After an interval of some twenty years the rarely used alternative of the earlier specimen may have become predominant, and the alternative originally predominant only recur as a reminiscence. In contemporary specimens a tendency in one to substitute angles where the other has curves must awaken suspicion. Where one group of examples is some twenty years the later the difference may be the natural result of the loss of freedom of hand which comes with old age, or even of specific disease. In such cases the conviction of an identity surviving amid difference often becomes a personal impression which it is difficult to transfer to others who have less experience of handwritings and their changes, and the most striking feature in Sir E. M. Thompson's book was the success with which this difficulty, and the kindred difficulty arising from change of mood, were combated. But without the production of more evidence the difficulties could not be entirely overcome, and it is important therefore to estimate what is the minimum effect which Sir E. M. Thompson's book of 1916 might be expected to have on any unprejudiced student who recognizes that the problem is one, not of the large and generous measure of identity we may demand in contemporary specimens claimed to be from the same hand, but of the much less patent identity which may be looked for in early and late specimens of a hand which has undergone both development and degradation.

If we think of the use which might be made of Sir E. M. Thompson's arguments in a trial at law it is obvious that they are much more valuable for defence than for attack. Let it be granted that if an estate were being claimed on the evidence adduced to show that the two hands are identical, a jury would probably refuse to award it. But reverse the case. Imagine the possessor of an estate challenged as to his right to it on the ground of the superficial *un*likeness of the hands, and Sir E. M. Thompson could hardly have failed to win his case for the defence; and this by itself is a great thing. If these three pages were not Shakespeare's work the dramatist to whom on the ground of style and temper I would most readily assign them (despite a difficulty about the date) would be ΅Thomas Heywood. But Heywood is definitely ruled out by his handwriting; that is to say, that if Sir Edward was right, even to this limited extent, Shakespeare survives a test which excludes Heywood, and not only Heywood but all the other dramatists of whose handwriting specimens are known to exist.

In the new study which he contributes to this volume Sir Edward carries his point still further, and also by his detailed examination of the forms of individual letters and by the illustrative plates which accompany the examination offers important help to students of Shakespeare's text who, as an aid to dealing with passages suspected of being corrupt, would like to begin by writing out the lines as nearly as may be as Shakespeare might have written them himself. As to these plates it should be noted that being copies, not facsimiles, they are not put forward as having any evidential value, or as superseding the complete facsimiles given in *Shakespeare's Handwriting*, and at the same time that they really possess high illustrative value as being based on a handwriting which (if not accepted as his) is at least more like to his than any other yet produced. Possibly some literary or epistolary specimen of Shakespeare's writing authenticated by a recognizable signature will yet be discovered and fulfil the confident expectation of some high authorities who, while regarding the evidence hitherto produced as inadequate, yet believe that if a satisfactory test is ever available Sir E. M. Thompson will be proved to be right. In the meantime the industry and ingenuity of Mr J. Dover Wilson have provided some corroborative evidence of an entirely new kind.

The carelessness of Elizabethan printers has been emphasized with wearisome frequency by Shakespeare editors for the best part of two centuries. In a good many instances, however, what are called misprints in the early editions of Shakespeare (and of other authors also) are not really misprints at all, but faults or slips in writing which the printer has faithfully reproduced. There was a time when any printer who was working on my own manuscript would tend to print an *n* where I had intended to write a *k*, turning *greek*, for instance, into *green*. It became evident to me that there was something misleading in the way I made a *k*, and a study of the misprints in the 'good quartos' of Shakespeare has made it evident to Mr Dover Wilson that there was something misleading in the way in which Shakespeare made several of his letters. In the letters *m*, *n*, *u* and combinations of these with each other and with *i* it is easy to make too few or too many strokes, and 'misprints' from this cause are common in the early texts of Shakespeare's; there are other misprints showing a similarity in the way he made the letters *c* and *i*, and again in the way he made *r* and *w*. Again, he must have made his *e* and *d* dangerously alike; also his *e* and *o*; also he must have had a way of making an *a* so that it could be mistaken for *or*. Therefore when Mr Wilson shows that there are instances of the letters named being written in the three pages not only in a way which suggested to him that a printer might easily misread them, but in a way which had actually led two such experienced students of Elizabethan writing as Sir E. M. Thompson and Dr W. W. Greg, when they were thinking only of the correct transliteration of the text, to produce the variants *momtanish* and *mountanish*, *Shrewsbury* and *Shrowsbury*, *ordere* and *orderd*, *or sorry* and *a sorry*, he makes a very considerable addition to the argument from handwriting.

According to Sir Sidney Lee (preface to 1922 edition of his *Life of William Shakespeare*, p. xiii) Elizabethan handwriting 'runs in a common mould which lacks clearly discernible traces of the writer's individuality.' Cockneys have been heard to say the same of sheep, and yet the shepherd knows each sheep in his flock from every other. Moreover, even with a very liberal admission of the existence of common features in the contemporary examples of the same style of writing, wherever agreement is found where difference is possible, it counts for something. To use a large *C* instead of a small one must have been so common a trick on account of the niggling form of the little *c* that the fact that Shakespeare and the writer of the three pages both clearly preferred the large letter proves very little; and yet it counts, since if only ten per cent. of contemporary playwrights were without this preference, yet if ten per cent. can be eliminated by this test, the field of choice is to this extent narrowed. The way of writing an *a* so that it looks like *or* narrows the field more than this, and when other common features are added, and we have to find a playwright with Shakespeare's attitude towards crowds, his attitude towards the monarchy, and his broad humanity, in whose handwriting these features also appear, but who is not Shakespeare, the task does not seem a very easy one.

We owe to Mr Dover Wilson new evidence as to yet another point in common between Shakespeare and the writer of the three pages; they both spelt in the same old-fashioned style. With the increased output of books spelling was being modernized very rapidly in the years (nearly a third of a century) which separate the More manuscript from the publication of the First Folio. The printers played a great part in this process, lagging behind the really modern spellers, but bringing the old-fashioned ones into some kind of harmony with them, except when the retention of some superfluous letter (mostly an *e*), or the use of *y* for *i*, made spacing easier. The spelling of the three pages abounds in old-fashioned forms; Mr Wilson is able to parallel them all from forms which have been preserved in the quarto editions of Shakespeare's plays, and it is in the highest degree unlikely that these were due either to the printer or to any intermediate copyist. Here then is another characteristic which must be discoverable in any playwright put forward as the author of the three pages. He must be an old-fashioned speller. The list seems to be getting rather long.

IV

As already noted, the original version of the episode of More's dealings with the long-haired serving-man was deleted, and variants substituted for

it. Over some of the deleted lines a piece of paper
was pasted and on this and the neighbouring margin
we find twenty-six lines written, in the hand Dr Greg
calls C, which begin with a Messenger's announce-
ment to More that the Lord Mayor and his wife are
coming to dine with him. Over against the stage
direction 'Enter A Messenger to moore' there is
written in the margin: 'Mess T. Goodal,' denoting
that the part of the messenger was to be played by an
actor of that name, who is known to us as one of
Lord Berkeley's players in 1581 and one of Lord
Strange's at the time that they acted the second part
of the *Seven Deadly Sins*, probably in or before 1590.
Until lately this was the only piece of evidence as to
the company for which the play was written and it
seemed to point decisively to that company being the
one for which Shakespeare wrote and acted. This
evidence still stands, and must still be reckoned with.
We can say with some certainty that if the play was
written before June 1594 it must have been written
for the company which it will be most convenient to
speak of as Shakespeare's, since the patrons who pro-
tected its members from being treated as rogues and
vagabonds changed with rather bewildering frequency
during the years with which the play has been, or may
be, connected. For reasons which are not very clear
this company became very large from about 1590 to
June 1594. During these years Edward Alleyn, the
most famous actor of his day, was playing for it,
though he retained his title 'the Lord Admiral's
servant.' The plague was bad in these years; the
theatres were very little open and many of the players
went touring in the provinces. When the plague had
subsided, in June 1594, the Lord Admiral's men were

reconstituted as a separate company, and in their first season made a great hit with a play called *The Wise Man of Westchester*, of which the book was the personal property of Alleyn, who only sold it to the company in 1601. In the summer of 1597 all the theatres were temporarily closed at the instance of the Lord Mayor, but the Admiral's men played again on October 11th, and they seem about this time to have been reinforced with members of another company (the Earl of Pembroke's) which had got itself into serious trouble. After this the company went on playing, but for whatever cause Alleyn temporarily retired about December 1597, and seems not to have returned to the stage till nearly the end of 1600. All these facts have to be stated because

(1) the writer of Dr Greg's 'hand C' in the play of *Sir Thomas More* has been lately identified by Dr Greg on the one hand, with the writer of the 'plot' of the *Seven Deadly Sins* (in which Goodal's name appears) for Shakespeare's company not later than 1590, and on the other hand, with the writer of a similar plot for the Admiral's men about 1597. Dr Greg also believes that the writing on the wrappers of the extant manuscripts of Munday's *John a Kent and John a Cumber* and of *Sir Thomas More* is his.

(2) Munday is known to have been writing for the Admiral's men in and after December 1597, and Dekker (in whose hand is an addition to the revised version of the episode of the long-haired serving-man) in and after January 1598. What Munday had been doing in the preceding years we do not know; that Dekker had previously been connected with Shakespeare's company is pretty certain, as he was arrested at its suit on 30 January 1599 (presumably

for some old debt) and released on payment of £3. 10s. by the Admiral's men.

(3) *The Wise Man of Westchester*, which made the success of the Admiral's season in 1594–5, has been connected by Fleay with Munday's *John a Kent and John a Cumber* which is concerned with the feats of the wizard John of Kent and his contest with John of Cumber and has its scene laid in and around Chester. If this connection holds (and it was accepted in his edition of Henslowe's Diary by Dr Greg, whom, since he is one of my witnesses, I must not contradict, even though he himself attaches no weight to the pronouncement), it seems fairly clear, since *The Wise Man of Westchester* continued to be so called in 1601, that the extant manuscript version in which the play is called on the wrapper *The Booke of John a Kent and John a Cumber* is the original form of the play and that Alleyn after acquiring it paid for it to be rewritten (not necessarily by Munday) under a new name, which accounts for Henslowe entering it in his Diary as 'Ne[w]' in 1594. Still, here we have Munday's play, if Fleay is to be held right, connected with the Admiral's men in 1594–95, and Munday and the writer of hand C further connected with them in 1597 and Dekker in January 1598. Are we to say that Goodal may have followed Alleyn when he left Shakespeare's company in 1594 and that *The Booke of Sir Thomas More* was written subsequently to June 1594 and for the Admiral's men and not for the company for which Shakespeare normally acted and wrote?

It is obvious at this point that the date of the play, or at least of the Additions to it, is now of increased importance. As long as the occurrence of Goodal's

name in one of the Additions stood alone it suggested
a date round about 1590. Now that three of the men
concerned in the manuscript are linked with a date
round about 1598 we have to consider rival possibilities. The dates which have been suggested cover
in all some fourteen years (1586–99) and there is the
further possibility to be reckoned with that the play
was drafted at one of the early dates and rewritten
with Additions at one of the later ones. Dyce, the
first editor of the play, dated it 'about 1590 or perhaps
a little earlier'; Richard Simpson brought it back to
'the last months of 1586, or the early months of
1587' on the score of the mention of an anti-alien
plot which was frustrated by the arrest of the youthful
conspirators (all under 21) in September 1586, cor-
roborated by the mention of Goodal and also (Greg,
†1006 and †1148) of Ogle, a theatrical property-
maker, who at present is known otherwise only by
entries in the Revels' accounts for 1572–3, and
1584–5; Dr Percy Simpson in reviewing Sir E. M.
Thompson's book in *The Library* for January
1917 drew attention to the grumble of the long-
haired servitor, Jack Faukner (Addition IV, 215 *sq.*)
'Moore had bin (*sic*) better a scowrd More ditch,
than a notcht mee thus' and suggested that the allusion would have had point 'just before the scouring
or just after the failure' of a cleansing which was
begun in May 1595. A date in or soon after 1595
had already been favoured by Fleay and others because of riots by apprentices and unruly youths in
June of that year. I may add also that in 1595
the price of butter reached 7*d.* as against an al-
leged standard price of 3*d.*, so that the danger
that it might go to 11*d.* referred to in the first

line of our three pages would have special point. Lastly, Professor E. H. C. Oliphant of Melbourne University, writing in the *Journal of English and Germanic Philology* in April 1919, favoured a date as late as 1598–9 on the ground that the style of Munday's share in the play suggests to him that it is later than his second *Robin Hood* play written in 1597–8 in collaboration with Chettle and earlier than *Sir John Oldcastle* written in 1599 in collaboration with Drayton, Hathwaye and Wilson. A date as late as this would also, he notes, suit very well for Dekker. Dr Greg, in his brief communication to the *Modern Language Review*, Jan. 1913, announcing the identity of the main hand in *Sir Thomas More* with that of Munday's *John a Kent* also favoured such a date from a momentary 'hallucination' (his own word) that the '...Decembris 1596' in the latter must be the date of composition. He and Sir E. M. Thompson are agreed in placing *More* between *John a Kent* and Munday's autograph dedication to his *The Heauen of the Mynde* which is dated 1602; but Sir Edward emphasizes his belief that *More* is nearer to *John a Kent*.

V

The recurrence of topical elements in Elizabethan plays has been so emphasized by various writers on the drama that it is not superfluous to point out that belief in it, when applied to riots in the streets of London, should be qualified by one obvious limitation. It is really not reasonable to believe that a play introducing a London riot would only have been written at some date when the playwrights would have run a risk of being hanged for their share in it. During any of the

fourteen years with which we are here concerned a
play with an anti-alien riot scene would have been
sure of crowded houses. I submit that after 24 July
1595 no company of actors would have dared to ask
for a licence to perform either *Sir Thomas More* or
any play with the 'ill May-day' of 1517 as an important episode in it. If anyone will be at the trouble
of reading the 1595 section of the Appendix to this
introduction he will see that in June of that year the
lads of London were in a very unruly mood. We
hear from Strype, but not from Stow, of a riot made
by 'poor Tradesmen' 'upon the strangers in Southwarke and other parts of the city' on June 12, and of
some 'young rioters' being committed to the Counter
and an attempted rescue (see Appendix: 1595). As
told by Stow himself the story is not of anti-alien
demonstrations, but of disturbances over the price of
butter and other provisions, for which other 'young
men' on June 27th were 'punished by whipping
setting in the pillorie and long imprisonment.' Two
days later on a Sunday afternoon there was a fresh
outbreak by 'a number of vnrulie youths' on Tower
Hill, followed by trouble between the Lord Mayor's
men and the warden of the Tower, which only the
tact of the Lord Mayor finally quelled. By this time
Elizabeth was thoroughly angry, and notified to the
Privy Council her pleasure that a Provost Marshal
should be appointed 'with sufficient authority to apprehend all such as should not be readily reformed
and corrected by the ordinarie officers of Iustice, and
that without delay to execute vpon the gallowes by
order of martiall law.' The provost marshal exercised
his powers with discretion; we do not hear of his
hanging anyone. But the Queen could be as cruel as

her father or her sister. Five of the 'unruly youths' arrested on Tower Hill were indicted, not for obstructing the police, but for high treason. When the trial came on at the Guildhall on July 22, it was held 'in presence of the Earle of Essex, and other sent from the Queene,' and under this pressure from the crown the lads 'were condemned of high treason, had iudgement to bee drawne, hanged, and quartered, and on the 24, of the same moneth they were drawne from Newgate to the tower-hill, and there executed accordingly.' I should not blame anyone not familiar with the manuscript and its additions for believing that, when it was known that these 'unruly youths' were in danger of such a fate, a play of *Sir Thomas More* was furbished up and the 'Johannes factotum' of the day drawn in to help, in order by exaggerating Henry VIII's clemency after the 'ill May-day,' exalting the royal authority, hinting that the mob had been promised a pardon (as the 1595 mob may have been by the Lord Mayor), to create an atmosphere and expectation of mercy by which the Queen might have been moved. Against such a theory there are a host of dull reasons as to the time available, the nature of other of the Additions and the plotting of the play as a whole; also in place of Tilney's scoldings the players would have been lucky, had they been so bold, if they were lodged in no worse place than the Counter. But it would have been a high adventure, and I'd like to believe it, and that Shakespeare took his risk like a man. But that after the Queen had wreaked this really savage vengeance—and that it was felt to be savage is shown by the repeated insistence on the rioters' youth—players and playwrights should try to get a licence for a play in which

Henry VIII's clemency would inevitably be contrasted by the spectators with his daughter's cruelty, and the hope of mercy abundantly held out by More would inevitably be taken as implying that the same hope had been held out by the Lord Mayor, is to me frankly and entirely incredible. I cannot believe that after those five lads were hanged and quartered as traitors on Tower Hill on 24 July 1595 there was any possibility of such a play being written; on the contrary, I believe that the play, as we have it, was recognized as dead and that seventeen months later it was sold to an amateur of such literature along with *John a Kent*.

When a street is gutted by a fire there is small temptation to play with the flames. With a bonfire, when it is not too big, it is another matter. All through Elizabeth's reign there must have been a risk of anti-alien outbreaks, as from France and Holland there came numerous immigrants, and though in most cases their original motives were to escape persecution, religious or political, these became, not only useful craftsmen, but keen traders, on whom many Londoners looked askance, under the belief that they enjoyed greater privileges than themselves. The trouble in 1586 which led Richard Simpson to assign the composition of *More* to that or the following year seems to have been crushed before it came to a head; popular feeling was concentrated in anger on the Babington conspiracy, and the Queen's birthday became the occasion of great demonstrations of loyalty. There is no mention of anti-alien riots in Holinshed or Stow, and there is nothing whatever in favour of this date for the play in any form, while the occurrence of Dekker's hand in the Additions makes it impossible for these. It has been assumed by writers on our play that the next outbreak was in 1595, but in May 1593 there were 'complaints and libels' against the Flemings and French which very seriously engaged the attention of the Queen's advisers, as will be seen in the two abstracts by Strype from papers belonging to Lord Halifax, quoted in my Appendix. The complaints were directed against the strangers acting as retail tradesmen, and two accounts were taken of their numbers, the ward authorities returning a total of 4300, while their own ministers reduced this to 3325. While these enquiries were making, 'libels' were posted up both in prose and verse, the former bidding the strangers depart out of the realm between this and the 9th of July next, and ending 'Apprentices will rise, to the number of 2336, and all the Apprentices and Journeymen will down with the Flemings and strangers.' Of the rhyme, posted up on the night of May 5th and brought to the constable and the rest of the watch by some of the inhabitants of the ward (oh, that Shakespeare could have given his version of the scene!), only the first four lines are quoted. 'The Court upon these seditious Motions, took the most prudent Measures to protect the poor Strangers and prevent any Riot or Insurrection. Several young men were taken up and examined about the confederacy to rise and drive out the strangers, and some of these rioters were put into the stocks, carted and whipt; for a terror to other Apprentices and Servants.' But the precautions taken were mostly secret and only the Lord Mayor 'and discreetest Aldermen' were informed of the real nature of the trouble. On the other hand, the complaints of the tradesmen, the counting of the aliens and the fact of the discovery of

the libels must all have been common talk in May
1593, and if the secrecy with which precautions
against a rising were taken led to a belief that no very
serious view was taken of the matter, here, I submit
was just the combination of events and popular feeling
which playwrights might try to exploit by reviving
the memory of the famous riots of 1517, without
seeming to themselves to run any exceptional risk.

As far then as our knowledge of the history of
London during our period extends the events of May
1593 seem specially full of suggestions for Munday
and his fellow dramatists and deceptively free from
any special warning of the fate which a play with an
anti-alien riot scene was certain to meet[1]. The anti-
alien movement came to the surface, which it does not
seem to have done in 1586; it was exclusively an anti-
alien movement which was certainly not the case in
1595; and it provoked no such drastically deterrent
punishment. I must confess that I cannot quote the
price of butter in this year. It had been 5*d*. and 6*d*.
a pound in 1591, and as it was 5*d*. and 7*d*. in 1595, it
was probably high enough in the intermediate year to
be a grievance. As to Moor Ditch, since the City
Fathers levied two-fifteenths to cleanse it in 1595 and
it had not been cleansed since 1569 we may be sure
that in 1593 it smelt quite badly enough to be talked
about. Until a date more inspiring to the playwrights
can be produced I think we may be content with this,
and as regards our evidence of other kinds it is

---

1 It has been asked why the riot scenes in More should have
been forbidden while those of Jack Straw and Jack Cade were
allowed to pass. The answer is surely that the city could be
trusted to protect the Court, in protecting itself, from an in-
vasion of 'foreigners' from Kent or Essex, or elsewhere, but
riots about its own grievances were another matter.

remarkable how it enables us to fit everything in. It is late enough for Shakespeare to have made his mark as a master of the humours of crowds by his handling of the Jack Cade scenes in the first revision of Part 2 of *Henry VI*[1]. It is late enough for there to be nothing improbable in Dekker having been allowed to try his 'prentice hand on a single episode in it[2]. It is late enough, again, for Munday's play of *John a Kent and John a Cumber* to be two or three years earlier, as the handwriting suggests. On the other hand, late in 1593 or early in 1594 (and we must allow some months for the play to have gone through all the stages[3] which can be traced) would not take us incon-

---

[1] This found its way into print in 1594, having been entered on the Stationers' Register in March as *The first part of the Contention*. I may note that I am quite content to be no more (and no less) certain of Shakespeare's authorship of our three pages than of his authorship of the Jack Cade scenes.

[2] Dekker is found writing for the Admiral's men in and after January, 1598. He had almost certainly had business connections before this with Shakespeare's company, as in January 1599 he was arrested for debt at their suit, and ransomed by his new employers. It may be worth noting that in his first entry of his name Henslowe spells it 'Dickers' and in the second entry 'Dicker.' Now a 'Thomas Dycker, gent' had a daughter Dorcas christened at St Giles', Cripplegate, on 27 October 1594 (*D.N.B.*). There is no proof that this was our Thomas Dekker, but it seems likely.

[3] The Additions are, of course, later than Munday's fair copy, and Munday's fair copy of scene i shows signs of being a prose revision of a scene originally in verse. There is nothing in the tone of the prose, in so far as it is prose, to provoke a playwright to drop unconsciously into decasyllabics, and yet here are a dozen to be accounted for: Thou art my prize and I pleade purchase of thee.—Thou thinkst thou hast the Goldsmithes wife in hand.—Are Piggions meate for a coorse Carpenter?—We may not, Betts; be pacient and heare more.—Were I not curbd by dutie and obedience.—Hands off proude

veniently far away from the occurrence of Goodal's
name in the plot of the *Seven Deadly Sins*, or even
from the latest known mention of Ogle the wigmaker. Finally, if the play was submitted to the
censor and his discouraging instructions received
early in 1594, about the time when Shakespeare's
company was returning from the long tour forced on
it by the closing of the theatres owing to the plague,
we may believe that *John a Kent* (just brought back
from touring) and *More* were put into their amateur
parchment wrappers from bits of the same manuscript
and inscribed by the owner of hand C, preparatory to
their being handed over to Alleyn, 'the servant of the
Lord High Admiral,' when in June 1594 his connection with Shakespeare's company came to an end,
and the Admiral's men once more played as a separate
company. If Fleay was right *John a Kent and John
a Cumber* was a good bargain, as in its revised form
The Wise Man of Westchester it was a great success
in 1594-5. In its original form I believe that Alleyn
sold it to an amateur of plays in December 1596, and
that the Queen's cruelty in hanging and quartering
the five 'unruly youths' for high treason in July
1595, having made the improbability of any revision

stranger or [by] him that bought me.—Mistresse I say you
shall along with me.—Ile call so many women to myne assistance, as weele not leave an inche vntorne of thee.—Brideled by
law and forced to bear your wrongs.—I am ashamed that free
borne Englishmen.—Should thus be brau'de and abusde by
them at home.

I should judge that in its first form this scene was Munday's
and that it was rewritten by B and copied again by Munday.
There may have been some interval between Munday's draft
and the revision, but when revision began I think it must have
been fairly continuous, as the playwrights seem partly to have
been revising their own work.

of *Sir Thomas More* sufficing to procure it a licence at last fully obvious, the 'Booke' of this was sold at the same time and to the same purchaser, though the untidy condition of the MS. and its lack of success discouraged him from recording the date of purchase as he did in *John a Kent*.

As against the second alternative date, late in 1595 or early in 1596, I have already done my best to show that the riots of that year and their sequel make these months not specially probable, but specially improbable. Mr Fleay's explanation of the instructions to delete the lines as to Bishop Fisher being sent to the Tower by finding in them a dangerous allusion to the Earl of Hertford being sent there in October 1595 is surely unhappy. Fisher was sent to the Tower for denying the royal supremacy in matters ecclesiastical, and as Elizabeth claimed and exercised this supremacy the censor's alarm needs no other explanation.

As for Professor Oliphant's suggestion of 1599 as the date of the composition of *More*[1] I will say no more as to the development of Munday's style than that in cases of multiple authorship such an argument seems doubly dangerous, as assuming certainty for the proposed attributions of the several scenes and ignoring the natural difference between a man's style when working alone and when working in collaboration. So late a date as 1599, moreover, takes us fifteen years away from the last mention of Ogle the wigmaker and some ten years away from the last mention of Goodal. It offers no explanation of the date, '...Decembris 1596,' or how *John a Kent* and *More* came to be bound in bits of the same manuscript. Lastly,

[1] For a discussion of Dr Schucking's arguments for a still later date, see Professor Chambers' contribution, p. 144.

it assigns the play to the period when Alleyn had temporarily left the stage (October 1597 to 1600). Though Professor Oliphant is a fellow-believer in Shakespeare's authorship of the three pages, and in other respects has done good work for the cause, I cannot fight under his banner in this respect. If *More* can be proved to be as late as 1599 I should regard the date as an obstacle to Shakespeare's authorship of the three pages so great as to be almost fatal. I say 'almost' fatal advisedly, because the other evidence produced by Sir E. M. Thompson and Mr Dover Wilson seems to me so strong that in spite of obvious difficulties I should be unable wholly to dismiss it. And if I were tempted to dismiss it, the next time I read the three pages I should become a lapsed heretic. Contemporary history, both of the theatres and the streets, helps our attribution; the handwriting helps it; Mr Dover Wilson's arguments from misprints and spelling help it. But to me personally the alpha and omega of the case is that in these three pages we have the tone and the temper of Shakespeare and of no other Elizabethan dramatist I have read.

I had written as far as this when, as a result of a chance conversation with Dr Greg, Professor R. W. Chambers came to reinforce our little company of upholders of Shakespeare's authorship of the 'three pages.' By contributing the last of the papers here printed Professor Chambers has provided a reasoned basis for the conviction expressed in my last paragraph on the ground of 'general impression.' He first shows that the remarkable resemblance between the passages on order and authority in *More*, in *Troilus and Cressida* and in *Coriolanus* is due not to copying or imitation but to the same mind reacting, at long intervals, in the same way to the same ideas, and he quotes other instances of resemblances between early and late plays of Shakespeare only explainable along these lines. As Professor Chambers develops his analysis of Shakespeare's attitude to crowds the three pages appear no longer in need of defence as Shakespeare's; they become explanatory of this attitude, revealing Shakespeare's humorous sympathy with the puzzled minds of men in the street, a sympathy which in other passages has been misinterpreted as mere ridicule and scorn. To show that we can understand Shakespeare better when we allow the three pages to take their modest place in Shakespeare's work crowns and completes all other methods of proof, and this final paper has notably increased my hope that the contributions which I have had the honour of bringing together and thus introducing may be held collectively to have proved their case.

I. APPENDIX

ACCOUNTS OF THE ANTI-ALIEN DIS-TURBANCES OF 1595, 1586 AND 1593 FROM CONTEMPORARY DOCUMENTS

1595

HERE are the events of 1595 (i.e. Ladyday 1595–Ladyday 1596) as recorded in the 1605 edition of Stowe's *Annales of England*, and the 1607 edition of *The Abridgement or Summarie of the English Chronicle*, 'first collected by master Iohn Stow, and after him augmented with sundry memorable Antiquities, and continued with maters forrein and domesticall, vnto this present yeare 1607. By E. H. Gentleman,' i.e. Edmond Howes who signs the address 'To the Honest and friendly Reader.' In the case of each event recorded we quote the fuller account.

1595. In the moneth of May after the grant of two fifteenes towardes the cleansing of the towne ditch: the same was begunne to be cast from Moregate towardes Bishopsgate, where that worke was ended.

Abridgement, p. 499.

This yeere by meanes of the late transporting of graine into forraine countries, the same was here growen to an excessiue price, as in some places from fourteene shillings to foure markes the quarter, and more, as the poore did feele, for all thinges els, what soeuer was sustenance for man, was likewise raised without all conscience and reason. ...Some prentises and other yoong people about the citie of London, being pinched of their victuals, more then they had beene accustomed, tooke from the market people in Southwarke, butter for their money, paying for the same but 3*d*. the pound, wheras the owners would haue had 5*d*. For the which disorder, the said yoong men, on the 27. of June were punished by whipping, setting on the pillorie and long imprisonment....The 29. of June, being Sunday in the afternoone, a number of vnrulie youths on the tower hill, being blamed by the warders of Tower street ward, threw at them stones, and draue them backe into Tower streete, being hartened thereunto by sounding of a trumpet, but the trumpeter hauing been a soldier, and many other of that companie were taken by the sherifs of London and sent to prison. About 7. of the clocke the same night, sir John Spencer lord maior rode to the tower hill, attended by his officers and others, to see the hill cleared of all tumultuous persons, where, about the middle of the hill, some warders of the tower, and lieutenants men being there, tolde the maior, that the sword ought not in that place to be borne up, and therefore two or three of them catching hold of the sworde, some bickering there was, and the sworde bearer with other hurt and wounded: but the lord maior, by his wise and discreete pacification, as also by proclamation in her maiesties name, in short time, cleared the hill of all trouble, and rode backe, the sworde bearer bearing up the sword before him.

The Queenes maiestie being informed of these, and sundry other disorders committed in & about her city of London, by vnlawful assemblies: And some attempting to rescue out of the hands of publike officers such as had bin lawfully arrested, whereby the peace had bin violated and broken: Her maiestie, for reformation thereof, by proclamation dated the 4. of July, straightly charged all her officers, both in the city, and places neere adioining in the counties of Midlesex, Kent, Surrey and Essex, that had authority to preserue the peace, and to punish offenders, more diligently, to the best of their powers, see to the suppression of all offenders against the peace, vpon paine to be not only remooued from their offices, but to be also punished as persons maintaining or comforting such offenders. And because the late vnlawfull assemblies & routs were compounded of sundry sorts of base people, some prentises, and some others wandring, idle persons of condition Rogues & vagabonds, and some colouring their wandring by the name of souldiers, her maiesty, for better direction to her officers of Iustice, and inquisition to be made, notified her pleasure to her councell to prescribe orders to be published, and straightly obserued, and for that purpose a Prouost marshall with sufficient authority to apprehend all such as should not be readily reformed and corrected by the ordinarie officers of Iustice, and that without delay to execute vpon the gallowes by order of martiall law. The orders prescribed, were the same day also by proclamation published. Sir Th. Wilford knight, was appointed prouost marshal for the time, he rode about, and through the City of London daily, with a number of men on horsebacke, armed, with their cases of pistols &c. This marshal apprehended many vagrant and idle people, brought them before the iustices, who committed them to diuers prisons. On the 22. of July were arraigned[1] in the Guildhall of London 5. of those vnruly youths that were apprehended on the Tower hill, they were condemned of high treason, had iudgement to bee drawne, hanged, and quartered, and on the 24. of the same moneth they were drawne from Newgate to the tower hill, and there executed accordingly.

In this time of dearth and scarcity of victuals, at London, an hens eg was sold for a peny, or three egs for two pence at the most, a pound of sweet butter at 7d. and so the like of fish or flesh, exceeding measure in price, such was our sins deseruing it.   *Annales*, pp. 1279–1281.

This yeare in February, 1595 [i.e. 1595/96], the Lord Maior and Aldermen, as well for expelling vagrant people out of the Cittie, reforming of common abuses to be aiding to the Clarks of the market, for redresse of Forrainers false

---

[1] The *Abridgement* adds, 'in presence of the Earle of Essex, and other sent from the Queene.'

waightes and measures, as to be assistant vnto all Constables, and other ciuil officers for the more speedy suppression of any distemperature that may arise by youth, or otherwayes: they ordained two Marshals, vz. Maister Reade, and Maister Simpson, and after them M. Roger Walrond was admitted alone. *Abridgement*, p. 502.

In the year 1595 the poor Tradesmen made a riot upon the Strangers in *Southwark*, and other Parts of the City of *London*; whereupon was a Presentment of the great Inquest for the said Borough, concerning the outragious Tumult and Disorder unjustly committed there upon *Thursday June* 12, 1595, and the Leaders were punished, and also the chief Offenders.

The like Tumults began at the same time within the *Liberties* (as they are called) where such Strangers commonly harboured. And upon the Complaint of the Elders of the *Dutch* and *French* Churches, Sir John Spencer, Lord Maior, committed some young Rioters to the Counter. And when some of their Fellow-Apprentices and Servants gathered in a Body, and attempted to break open the Counter, and deliver the Prisoners, the Maior went out in Person, and took twenty, or more of them, and committed all to safe Custody; and promised to proceed against them with all Severity, as he signified in a Letter to the Lord Keeper, dated 12th of June, 1595.

A Survey of the Cities of London and Westminster. By John Stow. Very much enlarged by John Strype. London, 1720. Vol. II. p. 303. Part of a chapter on 'Strangers settled in London.'

1586

RECORDER FLETEWODE TO LORD BURGHLEY[1].

Right honourable and my singular good Lord, this present daie, from two of the clocke untill six, my Lord Maior with some of his brethren, th' Aldermen, and myselfe, dyd examyne certaine apprentices for conspiring an insurrection in this cittie against the Frenche and Dutche, but speciallie against the Frenche, all things as lyke unto Yll May Daye, as could be devised in all manner of cyrcumstances, *mutatis mutandis*; they wanted nothing but execution. We have taken fyve, all of an age, yet all under 21, four of them Darbishire borne, the fyfte borne in Norhamshire. We are searching and seeking for the principall captayne. We hope we shall heare of him this present night, for he hath bene working all this day in the Whyt Hall at Westminster, and at his coming home we trust to have him. We have this night sett a standing watche armed from nyne untill seven in the morninge, and do meane to contynue so long as it shall be thought convenient unto your Honor, and the resydue of my Lords.

Mr. Alderman Woodcocke, who marryed the wydowe of Mr. Lanyson, shall be buried uppon Mondaye next. Sir Rowland Hayward is extreme sicke, and greatly distressed (our Lord comfort him!); my Ladie his wife is likewise verie sicke.

This night Mr. Attorney Generall sent his man unto me to sett my hand and seale unto a warrant to summon a quest of enquirie to appeare tomorrow at Westminster Hall. The citizens when they shall heare of it, will lyke thereof verie well, for they all crye owt that justice may be done uppon those traitors[2].

[1] Quoted from Thomas Wright's *Queen Elizabeth and her times* (1838), II. 308.
[2] The persons concerned in Babington's conspiracy. [Wright's note.]

The foresaid apprentices, being of the mysterie of plasterers, are commytted unto Newgate uppon the Quenes Highnes and her counsells comandement, where they are lyke to remayne, untyll they be delivered by speciall warrant. Here is presentlie no other thing worthie of writing. Wherefore I beseech God to preserve first her Majestie, and then your Lordship, from all those traitors and such other wicked people.

From the Guylde Hall, this present Tewesdaie, the sixt of September, at seven of the clocke in the eveninge, 1586.

Your Lordships most humblie bounden,
W. FLETEWODE.

At the sending away of my man this Weddensday morning, all the bells of London do ring for joye, that, upon the 7th of this monethe, being as this daie, Ao. 25, H. 8, her Grace was borne. There will be this daie but specially great feastings at supper. I have been bidden owt this night to supper in six or seven places.

1593

From John Strype's *Brief Annals of the Church and State under the reign of Queen Elizabeth,* being a continuation of the *Annals of the Church of England.* Vol. IV. London, 1731.

Num. CVII.

Strangers, Flemings *and* French *in the City of* London. *And Complaints of them and Libels against them; Anno* 1593. MSS. Car. D. Hallifax.

They contented not themselves with Manufactures, and Ware-Houses, but would keep Shops, and retail all manner of Goods. The *English* Shopkeepers made several Complaints and Remonstrances against them. Whereupon a strict Account was taken in every Ward of all Strangers inhabiting within *London*, with their Servants and Children. And Certificates were returned the 4th of *May*. When the Total of all the Strangers, with their Children and Servants, born out of the Realm, were 4300. Of which 267 were Denizons.

Another Scrutiny was made the same Year, 1593, by Order of the Chief Magistrates. Which was done by the Ministers and chief Officers of the Foreign Churches in *London*, and in the same Month of *May*. By which the Number of the Strangers of the *French*, *Dutch* and *Italian* Churches, did amount to 3325. Whereof 212 were found to be *English* born.

Complaint of them.

The Artificers *Freemen* within the City and Suburbs in *London*, made Complaint, by several Petitions, against the Trades and occupations exercised by Strangers. And upon due Information the Housholds appeared to be only 698

Libels set out against the Strangers.

While these Enquiries were making, to incense the People against them, there were these Lines in one of their Libels.

'Doth not the World see, that you, beastly Brutes, the *Belgians*, or rather Drunken Drones, and faint-hearted *Flemings*; and you, fraudulent *Father*, *Frenchmen*, by your cowardly Flight from your own natural Countries, have abandoned the same into the Hands of your proud, cowardly Enemies, and have by a feigned Hypocrisy, and counterfeit shew of Religion, placed yourselves in a most fertile Soil, under a most gracious and merciful Prince. Who hath been contented, to the great Prejudice of her own natural Subjects, to suffer you to live here in better Case and more Freedom, than her own People.—Be it known to all *Flemings* and *Frenchmen*, that it is best for them to depart out of the Realm of *England*, between this and the 9th of *July* next. If not, then to take that which follows. For that there shall be many a sore Stripe. Apprentices will rise, to the number of 2336. And all the Apprentices and Journeymen will down with the *Flemings* and Strangers.'

Num. cviii.

A Rhime set up against the Wall of the Dutch *Church-yard, on* Thursday May *the 5th, between Eleven and Twelve at Night. And there found by some of the Inhabitants of that Place; and brought to the Constable, and the rest of the Watch. Beginning,*

> *You, Strangers, that inhabit in this Land,*
> *Note this same Writing, do it understand.*
> *Conceive it well, for Safe-guard of your Lives,*
> *Your Goods, your Children and your dearest Wives.*

The Court, upon these seditious Motions, took the most prudent Measures to protect the poor Strangers and to prevent any Riot or Insurrection: Sending for the Lord Mayor and Aldermen; resolving that no open Notification should be given, but a private Admonition only, to the Mayor and discreetest Aldermen. And they not to know the Cause of their sending for. Orders to be given to them to appoint a strong Watch of Merchants and others, and like handicrafted Masters, to answer for their Apprentices and Servants Misdoing. The Subsidy-Books for *London* and the Suburbs, to be seen: how many Masters, and how many Men, and of what Trades, and if they use double Trades. The Preachers of their Churches to forewarn them of double Trades. And such as be of no Church to be avoided hence. And a Proclamation of these Things to be made publickly in *Guild-Hall*.

After these Orders from the Council Boards, several young Men were taken up, and examined about the Confederacy to rise, and drive out the Strangers—Some of these Rioters were put into the Stocks, carted and whipt; for a Terror to other Apprentices and Servants.

MSS. Car. D. Hallifax.

II. THE HANDWRITINGS OF THE MANUSCRIPT

By W. W. Greg

§ 1. *The Distribution of the Hands.*

THE palæographical study of the *More* manuscript was first systematically undertaken in the Malone Society's edition of the play printed in 1911. The different hands in which the manuscript is written were there clearly distinguished and the portions contributed by each fully, and I believe accurately, set forth[1]. It will not be necessary here to do more than briefly summarize the facts.

The manuscript contains six different hands, exclusive of that of Edmund Tilney, the Master of the Revels, who, as censor, made certain notes and alterations and is probably also responsible for a few marginal marks. These hands the edition designates as S, that of the scribe of the original play, and A, B, C, D, E, those in which the additions are written. I shall use the same symbols in the following discussion, but shall for convenience use each tó designate indifferently the handwriting or the scribe that wrote it.

S is responsible for the whole of the original fair draft of the play so far as it has survived (one or more leaves are missing after folio 5 and again after folio 11) but took no part in the revision. He wrote a well-

---

[1] On p. 67 the head-line inadvertently gives the hand as B instead of A, and at p. xviii, l. 28, C is a misprint for B.

formed and very regular hand with almost meticulous care, but it is distinctly of a literary rather than a professional type. The duplicate endings (the last nine lines were cancelled and rewritten in an expanded form) show that the writer, if not the author himself, at least worked under his immediate supervision. On the other hand, in l. 1847, the reading 'fashis', certainly a scribal error for 'fashiõ', is a mistake with which it is difficult to credit an author transcribing his own work. The few incidental alterations do not seem to afford evidence either way.

A writes nothing but folio 6ª (verso blank), which is clearly inserted in the wrong place. The addition belongs to scene xiii and is apparently intended to replace ll. 1471–1516 on folio 19ª, but it has never, it would seem, been definitely incorporated. It is unquestionably an author's draft, alterations being made *currente calamo*. It is in a general sense parallel to the original passage and borrows its first line therefrom, nor can I, for my part, detect any clear difference of style. Moreover, it is worth remark that one reason for the substitution would seem to have been the presence of an attack on 'the Prince' which might certainly be consi.'^red offensive, and that a somewhat similar though milder passage also appears in the revised version and is again cancelled.

B, an ill-formed current hand, appears in several additions of different sorts in different parts of the play. It is first found filling folio 7ª, the first page of an elaborate insertion which replaces a considerable section of the original draft. B's contribution is a slightly expanded version of the original scene iv which has been cancelled. Apart from such divergencies as would inevitably be introduced by a very careless scribe, the revision differs from the original mainly in the clown's part, the introduction of which appears to have been the motive of the substitution. This part is evidently the original composition of B, for he has added speeches by the same character subsequently, namely in the margin of scenes vi and vii (folios 10ᵃ–11ᵃ), but the slavish manner in which the rest is copied hardly suggests an author revising his own work[1]. Except for the marginal additions just mentioned, we do not meet B's work again for certain till we come to folio 16, which is entirely his. Here the first 67 lines form an

---

[1] The apparent improbability of the whole scene being transcribed, and so roughly transcribed, for the sake of introducing these few very poor speeches, has led to the suggestion that in this page we have the original draft of the scene in question substituted by the irate author for S's fair-copy, because the latter had ventured to suppress his vapid clown's part. This ingenious theory I feel bound to reject on various grounds. It is perhaps no strong objection that the revised scene is crowded onto one side of a leaf of paper, the verso of which was originally left blank. But on literary grounds alone it seems to me fairly clear that the clown's part is a later insertion—note the awkwardness of anticipating Lincoln's question in l. 57—and this view is confirmed by other considerations, for while there are no less than seven alterations made in the clown's part in the course of composition, there is not a single one in the rest of the scene. Further, it is difficult to suppose that the author in originally writing the scene would have fallen into the error of giving the speeches beginning at ll. 42 and 51 to Lincoln. The second of these blunders the writer himself noticed and corrected, but the earlier remained till altered by the substitution of the name 'Williā' by C in the course of the general revision. Both speeches are correctly ascribed by S. As to the motive for transcribing the whole, it should be observed that there is not very much room for insertion on folio 5ᵇ and also that the insertions and substitutions are more extensive, especially at the beginning, than those in scenes vi and vii.

addition at the end of scene ix of the original. This differs markedly from the earlier insertion, being throughout the original work of an author composing as he wrote: there are a number of alterations made *currente calamo*, and note that the speakers' names were added later, for ll. 21–35, which were cancelled as soon as written, are without them. Again, I cannot say that I detect any difference of style between the original scene and the addition. The last piece of B's handiwork, ll. 68–73 on folio 16^b, is the rough draft of a speech, intended as an introduction to the same original scene ix, which is found transcribed with other matter into its proper place by C[1].

C, the most extensive and most widely distributed of the revising hands, approaches more nearly than any other to the professional type both in caligraphic style and in the distinctive use of Italian script. In it are written no less than four and a half pages, two slips, and numerous marginal directions. This last fact, in conjunction with that already noticed, that C transcribes a rough draft by B, points to a play-house reviser and makes it unlikely that any of his work is original composition. We first find him con-tinuing the elaborate composite insertion begun by B on folio 7^a. On the verso of this leaf C writes a scene of which there is no trace in the original as it now stands, and at the foot of the page adds the stage-direction for another scene, which is then written by D on folios 8–9. In C's scene there are a few altera-

[1] Hand B should be compared with that of *The Captives*, &c., MS. Egerton 1994 (fols. 52–95) at the British Museum, which is presumably Thomas Heywood's. There is a considerable resemblance both in the writing and the spelling, but there are also differences which make it impossible to venture on an identification.

tions but not of a kind necessarily to imply authorship. C edits D (as he edited B) throughout his three pages, adding several of the speakers' names and apparently supplying half a line in one place. Subsequently C is found writing folios 12^a, 12^b, 13^a and the top half of 13^b. These three and a half pages contain a revision of scene viii, the original version of which is only partly preserved. The whole has been re-arranged, and a good deal has been rewritten, the Falkner-Morris portion being recast in prose. It is pretty clear, I think, that this revision was not the work of the original author, but neither is there any reason to ascribe it to C, whose slips appear to be those of a copyist rather than a composer. After these three and a half pages had been written, and folio 13^b completed by E, C fitted them into their place, supplying head and tail links on slips pasted on to the cancelled original pages, folios 11^b and 14^a. Of these, the second, as we have already seen, begins with some lines transcribed here by C from a rough draft by B. Whether B was the author of the whole link is uncertain, though it seems likely: that C was not appears from an evident error of transcription in l. 20.

D, the hand that writes three pages (folios 8^a, 8^b, and 9^a—9^b being blank) completing the composite insertion begun by B and C, supplies a revision of the beginning of scene vi, the original version of which is almost entirely lost. It is without question the hand of an author composing as he writes, probably with great fluency. The writing is in some respects careless and impatient: speakers' names are omitted or mis-written, and in one place, after complicated alteration and deletion, the passage was left in such a tangled state as to call for C's intervention.

The work of E is confined to the lower half of folio 13^b, on which he added an extension of the revised version of scene viii. There is not very much point in this supplement, which looks as though it had been added rather to fill up the blank half-page than for any weightier reason, a fact suggesting that it may well be an after-thought by the writer who effected the revision to which it is appended. The style appears to be identical. There is nothing to prove the addition autograph, but if we assume C's contribution to be a transcript it is natural to suppose that E is the hand of the revisional author.

The general lines of distinction between the six hands are quite clear, and I believe that the foregoing account may be accepted as correct. At the same time it is only fair to add that brief marginalia and alterations can often be only conjecturally assigned, and it must not be supposed that the identifications proposed in the Malone Society's edition are by any means all equally certain. Particularly it should be mentioned that hands C and D were once believed to be the same, and that although the weight of palæographical authority is at present certainly against this view, it has not yet been universally abandoned.

I am anxious not to lay any undue stress upon the evidence of authorship that can be deduced from handwriting, but I think that the following conclusions in regard to the additions are at least plausible. A is an author revising his own work. B on folio 7^a (scene iv) is transcribing with small original additions the work of another writer; on folio 16 (scene ix) he is making an addition to a scene originally written by himself. C is a transcriber only, copying on folio 7^b a new or revised scene by an unidentified author, on folios 12^a, 12^b, 13^a and part of 13^b a revision by E of an original scene (viii) by some other writer, and on the slips (folios 11^{*b} and 13^{*a}) links to the same scene written at any rate in part, and perhaps wholly, by B. D is a writer producing an entirely new version of a portion of scene vi originally written by the same author as scene iv. E is a writer making an addition to his own revision (transcribed by C) of another author's original scene viii. It follows, of course, if these inferences are correct, that the original version in hand S is not throughout the composition of a single author. This is a view that has lately been urged with considerable force by Mr Oliphant, whose work I shall have further occasion to mention.

Of the six hands under discussion, four can with greater or less confidence be identified with those either of known authors or of known documents, while the remaining two, A and B, are sufficiently individual to allow a hope that they too may be identified when the hands of the period come to be more widely studied. Meanwhile, we must be content with knowing that S is the writing of Anthony Munday and E of Thomas Dekker, that C also appears in certain dramatic 'plots' belonging to Lord Strange's and the Lord Admiral's companies, and that D may perhaps be the hand of Shakespeare himself.

§ 2. *The Identification of Hands* S, E, *and* C.

When discussing the hands in the Malone Society's edition of *More*, I came to the conclusion, for a reason already indicated, that the hand (S) in which the whole of the original fair draft of the play is written, was that of a scribe merely, that is of someone who was not himself the author of any part of it. Within a year the late J. S. Farmer issued a facsimile of the manuscript of *John a Kent and John a Cumber*, a play then in the possession of Lord Mostyn, which was seen at a glance to be in the same hand S of *More*. This play bears at the end the signature 'Anthony Mundy' and proved on investigation to be autograph throughout. The fact that Munday was well known as a dramatic author of course made the suggestion that in *More* he played the part of a mere scribe unreasonable, and in announcing the discovery in the *Modern Language Review* for January 1913 I certainly assumed him to have been the author of the original text, though I did not actually make the assertion. The inference was perhaps a natural one, but is not therefore to be excused, for it is clear that at most the facts established that Munday was at least part author. In the case of a piece written by several playwrights in collaboration it is likely that one of them would be charged with the task of preparing the fair-copy. Fortunately the error in my assumption was detected by Mr E. H. C. Oliphant, an ingenious Australian scholar, who, working on the hypothesis that more than one style was traceable in the original draft, published an interesting analysis of the play in the *Journal of English and Germanic Philology* for April 1919, which may very likely be on the right lines, even if it should need modification in detail.

The inference as to authorship was not the only mistake I made in drawing attention to the identity of handwriting in *More* and *John a Kent*. At the end of the latter play appears the fragmentary inscription '...Decembris 1596', concerning which I made the fortunately guarded remark: 'I am by no means certain that the date at the end of the play is autograph, though it is probably contemporary.' However, if the date is not autograph—and it probably is not—though we can, of course, say that the play was presumably not written after that year, it need not be contemporary except within wide limits. The importance of this lies in the fact that Munday's known autographs can be arranged in a chronological series. They are *John a Kent, Sir Thomas More*, and the preliminaries to his *Heaven of the Mind*, dated 22 December 1602, in Additional MS. 33384 at the British Museum. In the style of the writing *More* resembles each of the others more closely than these do one another, and must therefore occupy an intermediate position; while, *John a Kent* being not later than 1596 the order must be that given above. Relying on 1596 as approximately the date of the earlier play, I formerly suggested 1598–1600 as that of *More*, but since 1596 is really only a downward limit the date inferred from it can, of course, be no more.

The fallacy was pointed out by Sir Edward Maunde Thompson in a contribution to the Bibliographical Society's *Transactions* (1919, XIV. 325) on 'The Autograph Manuscripts of Anthony Mundy,' in which, by means of minute palæographical analysis, he was able not only to demonstrate the identity of the hand and the order of the manuscripts, but to suggest the relative length of the intervals that separate them, holding that 'while *More* is in a general sense intermediate between the other two MSS., it lies much closer chronologically to the earlier one.' It is very gratifying to find my perhaps hasty conclusion as to the order of the manuscripts thus confirmed by a veteran palæographer, and what he says concerning the relative intervals certainly accords with my own feeling on the subject. At the same time I am bound to say that the four pages written in 1602, doubtless at a sitting and in circumstances of which we are absolutely ignorant, afford rather poor evidence of the general character of Munday's hand at that date. Sir Edward proceeded to suggest, not however on purely palæographical grounds, that *John a Kent* may have been written about 1590 and *More* about 1592–3. These dates are certainly consistent with the evidence of handwriting, and may very possibly be correct; still I cannot feel, and I do not think that Sir Edward would himself maintain, that they rest on any very secure foundation.

But though certainty may be unattainable, speculation is not therefore idle, and it may be worth inquiring whether, assuming the 1602 autograph to be typical, the date of *John a Kent* must necessarily be placed before 1596[1]. The two hands certainly differ to a marked degree, but I do not think, allowing for

---

[1] In the case of so voluminous a writer as Munday there seems a good chance of further autographs coming to light, which may help to establish the character of that of 1602. I should like also to say that, while there is at present nothing to suggest that the date on *John a Kent* is autograph, I do not myself consider the suggestion as impossible as Sir Edward seems to think. The signature of the 1602 manuscript is clumsily written in what Sir Edward calls Munday's pseudo-Italian hand, while that at the end of *John a Kent* is in an ornate and flowing script which bears not the smallest resemblance to the other. But many writers had more than one style of signature, and there is no reason to doubt that in both instances Munday's name is autograph. In that case he was able, at least at the beginning of his career, to write a caligraphic style absolutely different from his ordinary hand, and I see no reason

the rapid development of a hand in constant practice
(a point on which Sir Edward lays stress), that we can
safely say that the change is greater than could have
taken place in the six years from December 1596 to
December 1602. At the same time *More* certainly
resembles the earlier hand much more closely than it
does the later, and it is probably safe to say that, unless
the writing of the 1602 manuscript is abnormal,
More cannot well be later than 1597–8, and that
should *John a Kent* prove to be before 1596, as it
well may, a correspondingly earlier date must be
assigned to *More*.

What has just been said applies, of course, to the
original version of the play as written by Munday.
But greater interest attaches to the question of the
date at which the revision took place, and before
passing on it is desirable to point out that, whenever
Munday may have performed his part, an early date
for the additions is somewhat discountenanced, though
not disproved, by another line of argument suggested,
but not fully developed, by Sir Edward. The two
plays clearly once belonged to the same company, for
they must have been bound at the same time since

to suppose that he was incapable of producing the exquisitely
written date, had he set himself to do so, though I do not
suggest that there is any reason to suppose that he did. (Compare the account of Dekker's hand below, p. 53.) I should add,
however, that while the signature seems in the same ink as the
text, that of the date is different, which makes it pretty certain
that it was a later addition. In connection with Munday's
signatures it may be remarked that the one reproduced in
Collier's *English Dramatic Poetry* (1831, III. 92, 1879, II. 474)
is not autograph but a forgery clumsily copied from a
memorandum by Dekker found among the accounts of Philip
Henslowe. Though Munday is frequently mentioned in the
famous Diary, his hand does not now appear in it.

portions of the same leaf of a thirteenth-century manuscript were used, and the covers were inscribed with the titles in the same theatrical hand[1]. Moreover, the very similar manner in which the two manuscripts have suffered from damp 'leaves little room for doubt that they must at some period have been laid aside together, in close contact with each other, and so remained undisturbed perhaps for years.' It is natural to suppose that it was during this period of neglect that the last leaf of *John a Kent* suffered the mutilation which has deprived us almost wholly of the end of the play, and in that case the dated inscription, which has shared in the damage, must, of course, have been made before the play was laid by. But the most natural 'cause of the neglect of the MS. of *Sir Thomas More*, in which its companion *John a Kent* was also involved,' would be its rejection—in revised form if my view is correct—by the censor. This then would point to the rejection and probably the revision likewise having taken place in 1596 at earliest. The argument, however, will clearly not bear pressing, for even supposing that the fortunes of the two manuscripts were as closely bound up with one another as Sir Edward plausibly assumes, it is, of course, not impossible that they may have knocked about in the chests of the company for some years before being consigned together to their 'damp limbo[2].'

[1] See below, p. 56.

[2] If it could be shown (as is not improbable) that the date December 1596 was that at which *John a Kent* passed out of the hands of its theatrical owners, the fact that the manuscript was then perfect and that it appears to have suffered in company with *More* would indicate 1596 as the downward, though not the upward, limit for the revision of the latter play.

That hand E was that of Thomas Dekker I never myself doubted, though the fact that I was unable to convince Sir George Warner of the certainty of the ascription induced me to refrain from positive assertion in the Malone Society's edition. It is pleasant to find that Sir Edward fully endorses my conjecture. So far as I am aware the only other examples of Dekker's handwriting of approximately the same date that survive are a number of short memoranda which he wrote in Henslowe's Diary[1]. They are as follows: 30 January 1598/9, acknowledgement of a loan of £3. 10s.; 1 August 1599, acknowledgement of a loan of £1; 10 May 1600, receipt for £3 in part payment of a play[2]; 5 May 1602, acknowledgement, jointly with Munday, of a debt of £5; there is also a signature of 19 December 1599. Dekker's hand varied widely. The signature is always in a flowing Italian script, which is also used throughout the first entry (that of 1598/9) and for the writer's name in the body of the second (1599). The bulk of the entry of 1602 on the other hand is in a bold English script, including the writer's name (the entry was not signed or more

    [1] One of these, that dated 1 August 1599, has been removed and is now preserved in the British Museum, Additional MS. 30262, fol. 66b. A letter at Dulwich from Dekker to Alleyn, dated 12 September 1616, is too late for useful comparison. The text is in English script, the signature in Italian, both easily recognizable in spite of the lapse of time. In another letter, undated but of the same period, the signature alone is autograph.
    [2] The entry, which is in Henslowe's hand, is subscribed: 'by John Day to the vse of Th Dekker Harry Chettle and himselfe'. Of this the first seven words are in one hand, presumably Day's, the remainder in another, probably Dekker's. This at least was Collier's view, and I now think that I was wrong in rejecting it in my edition of the Diary.

likely the signature has been cut away). All the rest, namely the entry of 1600 such as it is, and the dates of those of 1599 and 1602, together with Henslowe's name in the same, is in an Italian script, but one of a much clumsier type, not unlike what Sir Edward calls Munday's pseudo-Italian hand. Of Dekker's addition to the *More* manuscript the text is English, the speakers' names and directions pseudo-Italian.

The main interest of the entries lies in the possibility of tracing a progressive change in the English script. It is rather a subjective matter, but I seem to detect a certain development in breadth and flow as well as in pressure between August 1599 and May 1602 and a similar development between the writing in *More* and August 1599. There is, however, nothing to suggest that the *More* addition need be earlier than about 1597. Possibly, had the entry of 1598/9 been English, it might have helped towards a more definite conclusion.

One other point, however, is worth mention. The loan of £3. 10s. recorded on 30 January 1598/9 was for the purpose of discharging Dekker from the arrest of the Chamberlain's men (Diary, folio 53). From this we may reasonably infer that he had quarrelled with that company, but also that he had had relations with them at no very distant period. He is first known to have written for the Admiral's men for certain on 8 January 1597/8, and from this date he was kept for some years pretty constantly employed. We may, therefore, take 1597 as the latest year in which he can have been working for the Chamberlain's company. Munday is heard of in connection with the Admiral's men about the same time, his first payment being just before Christmas 1597.

Hand C I originally assigned to a playhouse reviser. Of this we now have further evidence. It appears, namely, that the same scribe also wrote the 'plot' of the *Seven Deadly Sins* preserved at Dulwich[1] and likewise a fragmentary 'plot' of an unidentified play in the British Museum (Additional MS. 10449, folio 4). Of these, the former belonged to the Strange-Chamberlain company and probably dates from 1591 at latest. The fragment, though the play to which it relates is not known, must from the cast have belonged to the Admiral's men and can, I believe, be dated as certainly before 16 November, and perhaps before 13 March, 1598, for reasons which I hope to publish shortly[2]. It follows that C, whoever he may have been, left the one company and joined the other probably between the beginning of 1591 and the end of 1597. There was a reconstruction of the Admiral's company in October 1597, and this may have been the occasion of his joining it. At the same time it is conceivable, though not, I think, likely, that the fragmentary plot may be earlier than this. If so, it would be reasonable to throw back C's migration to a considerably earlier period, and this is in any case quite possible. For there existed during the difficult years 1590–3 some close though rather obscure association between the two companies concerned, and it is tempting to imagine that C, originally a servant of Lord Strange, may have attached himself to Edward Alleyn and the Lord Admiral's men when the two companies started on their independent careers in the spring of 1594.

[1] There is a facsimile in W. Young's *History of Dulwich College*, 1889, II. 5.

[2] In an essay on the *Battle of Alcazar* for the Malone Society.

Each 'plot' was superscribed with the title of the play in large gothic letters partly surrounded with rough pen ornament. The writing and still more the ornament enable us to identify the similar super-scriptions on the vellum wrappers of *John a Kent* and *More* as being likewise written by C[1]. Unless I am mistaken C also wrote a few hasty directions in the margins of *John a Kent*.

Hand D having been allotted for special treatment to Sir Edward Maunde Thompson, it only remains for me to summarize the evidence for the date of the manuscript as a whole which I have been able to find. It will have been noticed how per-sistently different lines of argument point to 1597 as the *terminus ad quem* alike for the original draft and for the additions. This date may then, I think, be accepted as reasonably certain. But there is nothing to prevent the additions, and still more the original, having been written several years earlier, or to con-flict in any way with the date 1593–4 proposed in Mr Pollard's Introduction.

---

[1] Sir Edward remarks that the titles are 'not, apparently, in one hand, but in the same style.' I do not understand his hesitation.

PLATE I

No. 1

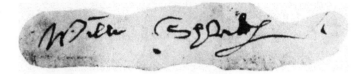

No. 2

No. 3

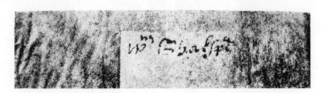

SHAKESPEARE'S SIGNATURES TO THREE LEGAL
DOCUMENTS, 1612, 1613

PLATE II

No. 4

No. 5

No. 6

SHAKESPEARE'S SIGNATURES TO THE THREE SHEETS OF HIS WILL, 1616

III. THE HANDWRITING OF THE THREE PAGES ATTRIBUTED TO SHAKESPEARE COMPARED WITH HIS SIGNATURES

By Sir E. Maunde Thompson, G.C.B.

WHEN I contributed, in 1916, to *Shakespeare's England*—the work compiled under the auspices of the Oxford University Press in celebration of the Tercentenary of the death of Shakespeare—a chapter on the 'Handwriting of England' at that period, I ventured to suggest that a close study of, and the resulting intimacy with, the English hand which Shakespeare wrote might be applied with a fair prospect of success to the solution of some of the doubtful passages in his plays. In the subsequent study on *Shakespeare's Handwriting*, in which I attempted to show that the handwriting of one of the Additions in the play of *Sir Thomas More*, now the Harleian MS. 7368 in the British Museum, is the handwriting of Shakespeare himself, I submitted an examination of the six surviving authentic signatures of the poet, and also of the handwriting of the Addition, in support of my contention. It has now been suggested that it would be of use to Shakespearian scholars if I were to analyse and compare still more closely the individual letters of these writings and record the results of such further study, and at the same time notice how imperfect and hurried writing may have affected the normal shapes of the letters and have led to confusion and misinterpretation, and how the grouping and linking of certain letters may have been misunderstood or misapplied. I have accordingly here attempted to follow this suggestion in a way which may be practically useful, accompanying my remarks with drawings of the letters and combinations referred to.

It will be convenient first to state briefly the position I have already taken up in regard to the six surviving signatures of Shakespeare, and to the three foolscap pages which contain the Addition to the play of *Sir Thomas More*, the composition of which has been ascribed to Shakespeare and which I have concluded to be in his autograph.

Shakespeare's Signatures

The six Signatures fall into two groups, of three in each group. The first group consists of signatures subscribed to: (1) Deposition in a lawsuit, 11th May 1612, now in the Public Record Office; (2) Conveyance of a house in Blackfriars, London, purchased by Shakespeare, 10th March 1613, now in the Guildhall Library; (3) Mortgage-deed of the same property, 11th March 1613, now in the British Museum. The second group consists of Shakespeare's three signatures on the three sheets of his will, executed 25th March, 1616, now in Somerset House. The signatures of the first group were subscribed when the writer was presumably in normal health; those of the second group, in his last illness.

All the signatures are written in the native English hand, and were subscribed within the last four years of Shakespeare's life, proving that at the close of his career he still wrote the English hand which, in his day, a Stratford boy would be taught at school.

There is a remarkable distinction to be noticed between the two groups. In the signatures of the first group the surname is written in a shortened form; in those of the second group it is written in full.

In the first group the earliest signature (No. 1) is that subscribed to the Deposition: Willm̄ Shakp. The letter p with a horizontal stroke passing through its stem may be read as per, or Shakespeare may (but not so probably) have used the cross-stroke as a general sign of abbreviation[1]. In the two Blackfriars deeds (Nos. 2 and 3) the surname is abbreviated in two different ways, each differing from No. 1. From the manner in which he executed these two deeds, it is evident that Shakespeare imagined that he was obliged, in each case, to confine his signature within the limits of the parchment label which is inserted in the foot of the deed to carry the seal, and not to allow it to trespass upon the parchment of the deed itself.

In No. 2 he has written his name in two lines (the surname below the Christian name), at first thus: William Shakspē, the surname ending close to the edge of the label and having above the e a flourish indicating abbreviation. The signature was thus in itself complete, in a shortened form which the writer was probably in the habit of using. But then, perhaps doubting whether the abbreviated name would suffice, he added the left-shouldered letter ƨ, thus altering the surname to Shakspēr (the abbreviating flourish being

---

[1] It is to be noticed that the method of crossing the stem by looping it is the same as that followed in the construction of the symbol for per or par in the Addition to the play of *Sir Thomas More*.

left standing above the now penultimate letter, instead of being in the proper position above the final letter, and thus without significance). That the ʒ is an addition is proved by the paler colour of the ink. Further, it was inserted with difficulty; for, while trying to satisfy his superstition for confining his signature to the label, on which he had left no clear room for any addition to the abbreviated surname already subscribed, Shakespeare was compelled to encroach, though ever so little, on the parchment of the deed by writing the upper portion of the ʒ upon it; yet he managed to draw back the lower half of the letter and ensconce it within the sacred boundary[1].

The Mortgage-deed is dated the day after the conveyance and would be executed on that day, or, if the modern practice then obtained in dealing with a transaction of this nature, simultaneously with the conveyance. After his recent trouble in trying to keep strictly to the label of the conveyance, Shakespeare now, subscribing his signature to the mortgage (No. 3), made sure of keeping it within limits by writing it, in a single line, in more careful style, not in his usual cursive writing as in No. 2, but in formal set letters: Wm Shakspē—with the same abbreviated form of surname which he had first employed in No. 2 before the addition of the ʒ.

The three signatures of the first group, then, prove that Shakespeare was in the habit of signing his surname, even in legal documents, in abbreviated form, but not always in the same form, though probably he

---

[1] The addition of the ʒ was noticed by Malone, *Inquiry into the authenticity of certain miscellaneous papers*, etc., 1796, p. 137 (with a facsimile of the signature), and described by him as written 'on the very edge of the label.'

had a preference for Shakspē. But these signatures do not only differ in spelling; they differ also in style of writing. The best written signature, inscribed with freedom, is No. 1. In No. 2 the writing shows less freedom, in part no doubt owing to confinement to limited space, and perhaps also to another cause which will be referred to below. No. 3 is in a formal hand and therefore is of less value than the other two cursively written specimens for determining the character of the poet's handwriting; and like No. 2, this signature also is wanting in freedom.

Turning now to the second group of signatures, viz. the three signatures inscribed respectively on the three sheets of Shakespeare's will (which may be referred to as Nos. 4, 5 and 6), the first two can be disposed of in a few words. They are merely the authenticating signatures attached to the first two sheets. They read: William Shakspere (No. 4), and Willm̄ Shakspere (No. 5).

The most important signature is No. 6, being the signature executing the will itself: 'By me William Shakspeare.' There can be little doubt that it was subscribed before Nos. 4 and 5. The first three words are written firmly and legibly; but, in attempting the surname the sick man's hand gave way. This failure to accomplish the signature successfully after beginning so well may primarily be attributed to Shakespeare's physical condition. When the will was placed before him, he was about to subscribe probably the most important signature of his life. No doubt, by a supreme effort he braced himself to the task, and, with the sense of the formality of the occasion strong upon him, he began to write, and to write very fairly well, in scrivener style, with the formal words 'By me.' Again under the same influence of formality, he even introduced among his letters certain ornamental preliminary up-strokes, such as we may therefore almost certainly assume he would habitually have used especially in formal scrivener's writing; and which we find abundantly employed in the Addition to the play of *Sir Thomas More*[1], but of which we have no instance in connection with his other signatures—and thus he succeeded in writing his Christian name. But then he came to an obstacle; his failing hand was evidently too weak to form correctly the difficult English *S* of his surname; his effort was exhausted, and the rest of the signature was finished with painful effort. I shall have occasion to recur to this failure. Here it is to be noted that he first wrote the surname in abbreviated form, Shakspē (as in No. 3, and as, at first, in No. 2), afterwards, however, adding the final letters *are* either on his own motion, or perhaps more probably on the lawyer's suggestion, in order to have the name in full. He then no doubt subscribed the authenticating signatures Nos. 4 and 5, not caring how he scrawled them, but in both cases spelling his surname without the *a* in the second syllable.

There is a notable point in connection with Shakespeare's signatures. He generally employed the Italian cursive long *s* (*ſ*) for the medial *s* of his surname: the only concession that he can be shown to have made to the new style. The native English long *s* (f) occurs in only one instance (No. 5).

[1] These upstrokes in the signature No. 6 and in the Addition are fully examined below, pp. 77–81.

Did Shakespeare suffer from writer's cramp?

The close of this general survey of the six authentic signatures of Shakespeare may be a fitting place to refer to opinions which have been entertained that in his later years he suffered from nervous disease which betrays itself in his handwriting. J. F. Nisbet in his book on *The Insanity of Genius* (1891) concludes, after examination of the signatures to the will, that Shakespeare's ailment was a prostration of the nervous system and that in his later days he was a victim to nerve disorder. In March 1919 the late Dr R. W. Leftwich delivered before the Royal Society of Medicine a lecture on 'The Evidence of disease in Shakespeare's handwriting' in which he analysed the signatures and decided that the writer was subject to the spastic or spasmodic form of writer's cramp. Without venturing to criticize these opinions, I may state that independently there had arisen in my mind, from the time when I first entered on an examination of Shakespeare's signatures, a suspicion that he had been afflicted with some nervous complaint which had left its mark upon his handwriting; and I propose to explain briefly the conclusion to which I have been led by the study of certain defects in those signatures.

The worst instances of failure, as we have already seen, are in the subscriptions to the will, namely, No. 6, the main signature, and Nos. 4 and 5, the two authenticating signatures of the first two sheets, of which No. 4 is too much defaced to be of any particular value. In the general description of the signatures I have noted that the defective writing of these three may be primarily accounted for by the

testator's weak physical condition. That Shakespeare
was stricken with sudden illness may be inferred from
the fact that the rough draft of the will was made use
of for execution, instead of waiting for a fair engross-
ment. But the question arises whether his illness
alone is to be held accountable for his failure in the
signatures or whether there was any other contributory
cause. He succeeded in writing the first three words
of the main signature (No. 6) 'By me William' very
legibly. The letters are a little irregular in details, but
there is no sign of any approaching collapse; and to all
appearance, if his state of health was alone concerned,
there was no reason why Shakespeare should not have
written his surname as successfully as the three preceding words. It was only when he came to attempt
the capital S of his surname—a difficult letter, under
any conditions, to write symmetrically—that his hand
gave way. It failed from inability to accomplish in a
normal manner the outer semicircular curve embracing the body of the letter, which leads off with
a reverse action of the hand moving from right to left.
The moment the hand begins to move leftwards to
form the base, the curve grows angular and, instead
of describing the semicircle clear of the enclosed letter,
the pen abruptly jerks upward, skirting the back of
the initial curve. Now I think that there can be little
doubt that this sudden failure was due to something
more than weakness of health, and moreover, that
Shakespeare was himself conscious of inability to control his hand when attempting a curve in reverse
action, as just described, under embarrassing conditions, as in the present execution of his will; and
hence that failure was inevitable. That he was conscious of this nervous inability I infer from the fact

that in the signature No. 5 he shirks the difficult moment of the curve by leaving a gap in the back of the embracing semicircle. The imperfect writing of the rest of the surname in No. 6 and of the two authenticating signatures Nos. 4 and 5 I would attribute to Shakespeare's nervous condition intensified by his failure with the capital *S* of No. 6.

If, then, Shakespeare was indeed conscious, at the time of his last illness, of a weakness in his handwriting, in other words that he was in his later years subject, in some unknown degree, to a form of writer's cramp; and if I am right in suggesting that his failure with signature No. 6 was not altogether attributable to illness, but also to a nervous disablement in signing his name—a form of cramp which is not uncommon with those who are affected in this way—we should look for any indication of the growth of the disease that may be found in his earlier signatures.

We return to the three signatures of the first group, written under normal conditions of health, and we will examine in each one the crucial point at which we have seen that Shakespeare's hand failed when executing his will—namely, the capital *S* of the surname. That letter in signature No. 1, both in regard to the actual body of the *S* and to the semicircle embracing the letter, is formed with perfect symmetry and evidently with a rapid and unembarrassed action of the hand in describing the alternating curves; so rapidly and lightly indeed did the pen travel, that the ink failed to follow its course throughout and left only a trace in a portion of the base-curve. Here there is no symptom of nervous disease. The signature was written in May 1612, nearly four years before the date of the will.

Ten months later, however, there exist, it seems to me, in the crucial capital *S* of both Blackfriars deeds (Nos. 2 and 3) sufficient indications of embarrassment to show that the writer was conscious of weakness of hand in forming that letter of alternating curves. It will be remembered that both signatures were written within the boundaries of the seal labels, and to some extent their faultiness may be attributed to the confined space. But for our present purpose we restrict our attention to the capital letter of the surname. Taking No. 2 in hand, and comparing that crucial letter with the symmetrically written letter in No. 1, we see how far it is wanting in the free and rapid movement of that example. It was evidently written slowly, and when the pen was brought round to effect the semicircular embracing curve, moving from right to left, there is weakness in the curve at the back of the letter, and again when, instead of finishing off with a symmetrical overhead cover, the arch of the embracing curve is brought down with a heavy pressure, like the lid of a box, on to the head of the letter. When Shakespeare proceeded to sign the mortgage-deed No. 3, either simultaneously with No. 2 or on the following day, he changed his style of writing; but again we see even greater weakness in the formation of the crucial capital *S*. The embracing curve at the back of the letter is carried upwards, hesitatingly, to a disproportionate height, and the covering arch ends off in a tremulous stroke. In these two signatures, then, we find a feeble and embarrassed treatment of the capital *S* of the surname and especially in the execution of the semicircular embracing curve of the letter at the very point at which the signature No. 6 of the will breaks down

PLATE III

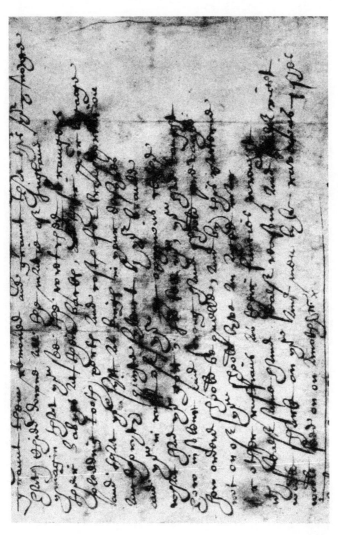

THE ADDITION (D) TO THE PLAY OF "SIR THOMAS MORE," LINES 72–87

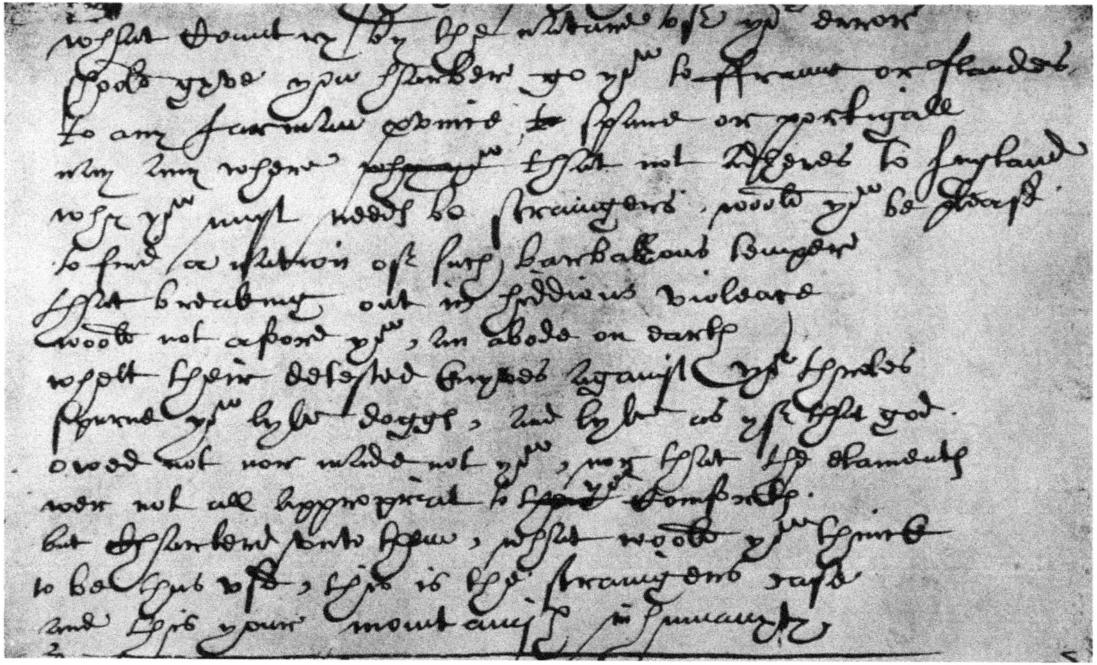

PLATE IV

THE ADDITION (D) TO THE PLAY OF "SIR THOMAS MORE," LINES 126–140

—a coincidence which, it seems, must be accounted for by some contributory cause other than mere temporary embarrassment, such as writing in confined space or in the presence of witnesses.

From what has been now stated, I think that sufficient evidence is afforded by defects in his signatures to show that, in the three years preceding the date of his death, Shakespeare experienced a difficulty in signing his name, arising from the growing disability to control the reverse action of the hand as above described; and as this action of the hand would be put in motion every time he wrote the initial letter of his surname, that letter would gradually come to be, so to say, the nerve-centre of the disease and the point at which his signature might break down. But it should not be assumed that such a form of writer's cramp would necessarily incapacitate him from fluent practice of the pen in an ordinary way, as in literary composition written at leisure and free from external disturbing embarrassments. It may have affected only the writing of his signature, and even then, possibly, only under conditions which might cause temporary nervousness and thus call into action the latent cramp at the crucial moment.

The Addition (D) to the play of 'Sir Thomas More'

This Addition, the composition of which has been attributed to Shakespeare, and which I submit is in his autograph, consists of 147 numbered lines written for insertion in a scene of the insurrection of Londoners against the aliens resident in the city, which was quelled by the intervention of More, then sheriff. The lines fill three of the pages of two inserted leaves (the verso side of the second leaf being left blank); but the lines numbered 94 and 95, the last lines of the second page, are double metrical lines, thus written in order to finish off a speech without carrying over its conclusion to the second leaf. The actual number of the metrical lines of the Addition is therefore 149. The first leaf has suffered severely from damp, which has injured the writing; the second leaf is perfect.

The Addition is written entirely by one hand, in the native cursive handwriting which was still the common character, taught in the schools and generally used in Shakespeare's time, and not yet superseded by the encroaching Italian cursive, which however was making its way in England as an alternative current hand. The English hand, cast by the scriveners and writing-masters into a uniform style, was the ' Secretary hand '—a term which came to be extended to the general cursive hand which in natural course assimilated individual modifications and changes in the forms of letters. It is in this freer 'Secretary hand' that the Addition is written; subject, however, in this instance, to a remarkable variation of style, shifting in sympathy with the character of the composition.

I may here briefly state my view regarding this variation of style, which I have already made known in the study on *Shakespeare's Handwriting*. There is a marked distinction between the writing of the first two pages of the Addition and that of the third page; the text of the former is evidently written with speed, the rapid action of the hand being indicated, for example, by the unusual length of the long-shafted descending letters and by a certain dash in the formation of others. These signs of speed generally slacken in the course of the second page, in which a more deliberate and heavier style supervenes—a change which seems to be coincident with the change in the character of the composition—the change from the noisy tumult of the insurgents to the intervention of More with his persuasive speeches requiring greater thought and choice of language. The full effect of this change in the style of the composition is made manifest in the yet more deliberate character of the writing of the third page. Here there is a stronger contrast between the light and heavy strokes than is the case generally in the first two pages, and long-shafted letters give place to others which are stoutly-shafted and even truncated. Of these two styles of writing, it may be assumed that the more deliberate style would represent the characteristic hand of the writer, being the style in which he would set down his more thoughtful scenes. There would be temporary pauses in the course of composition and corresponding suspensions of the pen and consequent loss in the momentum of the writing. In scenes of a lighter nature, on the other hand, he might be expected to compose so easily as to inscribe line after line, with little variety, in the ordinary scrivener's clerical style.

This liability to change of character under the transient influence of greater or less mental effort constitutes the most remarkable feature in the handwriting of the Addition; and changes in the actual formation of letters which may be attributed to this influence will be noted as we proceed with our study. This sensitiveness, we may add, could hardly have produced the result which is here so noteworthy, had not the handwriting been of an unusual fluency which could respond instantaneously to the moods of the writer. He was a skilful and experienced penman. When he is writing his scrivener's hand, its uniformity denotes long and constant practice; when he is writing his thoughtful author's hand, although this is formed rather roughly and without so much attention to uniformity, its flexibility and unrestraint equally indicate full practical command of a legible and workmanlike handwriting. In both styles he shows a disposition to play with his pen, to exaggerate pendent curves, and to finish off the final letters of his words in a flourish, more especially as he approaches the end of a line; and this tendency to flourish is more conspicuous in the deliberate than in the scrivener style, the pen there working at greater leisure and the writer having, so to say, more time to be fanciful in his calligraphy, and, in addition to flourishing, to give greater variety to his letters by emphasizing them with heavier downstrokes. The letter which is most frequently flourished at the end of a word is *e*, the loop being finished off with a curved tag terminating in a minute curl or dot. This flourished letter is so persistently, though not uniformly, used by the writer that it may be regarded as one of the particular forms by which his handwriting might be identified; and it is to be remarked that it seems to have been used in Shakespeare's signatures to his will, though their imperfect condition leaves its identification doubtful. The same curved flourish is also applied to other letters, such as *d* or *ll* at the end of a word. Again, the descending bow of final *y* or final *h*, at the end of a line, may terminate in a fanciful flourish; or the tag which emerges from the top of a final round *s* may be exaggerated into an extended up-stroke in the air. The practice, also followed by the writer, of lengthening the horizontal stroke forming a part of certain letters, such as the head-stroke of *c* or *g* or the cross-bar of *k* or *t*, when any such letter stands at the end of a word, is another similar indication of the writer's readiness to finish off his words in fanciful style. But all such flourishes, and also slack formation of curves in the bodies of words which may be almost called flourishes, are not to be counted as merely calligraphic eccentricities; for they may also be the unfortunate causes of misreadings of the letters or words which they affect.

Points of resemblance between the Signatures and the Addition

I may now briefly state the points of resemblance between the handwriting of Shakespeare's signatures and the handwriting of the Addition, both in the formation of letters and in other palæographical details, which I venture to think have justified me in my conclusion that the writer of the Addition was also the writer of the Signatures. To attempt to extract evidence from a scanty gleaning of signatures, the only authentic examples of Shakespeare's handwriting, all varying within themselves to a degree more perplexing than usual, and three of them imperfectly written in illness, might appear a hazardous undertaking. Moreover, the length of time which separates the writing of the Signatures from the writing of the Addition adds to the difficulties of comparison of the documents. The Signatures were all subscribed within the last four years, 1612–16, of Shakespeare's life. If we are to assign the Addition to A.D. 1593–4 there would remain an interval of nearly a score or more years during which changes may have taken place in details of Shakespeare's handwriting. But, notwithstanding an apparently unpromising case, evidence has been forthcoming having a cumulative value which, though it may not at once carry conviction, yet claims the right of being duly weighed.

The mere fact of any one or more letters being of the same character in two different specimens of handwriting of course does not prove that those documents were written by one and the same person. There must be something more than bare resemblance to justify identification—some peculiarity, some trick of the hand, which is to be recognized as just as personal as a peculiarity of feature or a trick of expression or manner. The first letter in Shakespeare's hand which satisfies the condition of possessing a peculiarity which may be regarded as personal is the open *a*, linked with the *h*, in the surname of signature No. 1. This letter (the construction of which is fully described below in the Analysis of Letters) is remarkable in being formed with a spur at the back, which is no essential part of it but seems to be a personal mark of this hand[1]. And when we turn to the Addition and find therein instances of the open *a* formed with the spur, we may regard its occurrence both in the Signatures and in the Addition as significant evidence of identity. Again, Shakespeare makes use in his few signatures

[1] I have kept a constant watch for the occurrence of this spur in the numerous documents of the period that have passed under my eyes, but I have never yet observed it in any, except in Shakespeare's Signature, No. 1, and in the Addition. I have also had the benefit of the valuable assistance of my old colleague Mr J. P. Gilson, keeper of the MSS. in the British Museum, who has kindly examined many collections of MSS. on my behalf.

of three out of the four forms of the latter *k* which
appear in the Addition; and yet again various shapes
which the letter *p* assumes in the Addition are found
also in the Signatures.

In regard to a certain form of the letter *p*, I have
to record an identification which I have only recently
made and which therefore does not appear in my
monograph on *Shakespeare's Handwriting*. Now at
length a connection is found between the handwriting of the Addition and the handwriting of
signature No. 3, which, it will be remembered, is
inscribed in a set, uncursive style, and which I therefore could hardly have expected to see represented in
the cursive lines of the Addition. In that MS. the first
page and the first few lines of the second are filled
with the tumultuous clamour of the rioters and their
leaders and the attempts of More and the authorities
to get a hearing. The text down to this point is
written in the lighter style which I have described
above as Shakespeare's scrivener hand, and is dashed
off rapidly without a stay. But then, at line 50, the
leaders of the mob intervene with the cry 'Peace,
peace, scilens, peace!'—and the first three words show
a sudden change in the style of writing: they are
written deliberately, and the stress of the pen is
heavier; and two of the letters of which they are
composed are of special set forms. These two forms
are also found in Shakespeare's deliberately written
signature, No. 3. The letters are *p* and *e*. The *p* is
a short, truncated letter, not unlike an ordinary
printer's Roman lower-case p, having a short vertical
stem commencing with a small hook or serif on the
left, then a short horizontal cross-bar is drawn to
form the base of the head-loop, which is completed

by the addition of the necessary curve[1]. The two initial *p*'s of the two words 'peace, peace' seem to be the only instances of this abnormal letter to be found in the Addition. One or two other letters bear a close resemblance to them, but they are indistinct and are probably only instances of the scrivener's normal short-stemmed *p*. The letter *e* employed in the three words is of the set form of the letter, composed of two disconnected concave curves, which is used only occasionally in the Addition. The letter *e* which stands at the end of the second word 'peace' is to be noticed on account of the flattening or extension, in a horizontal stroke, of the upper curve, such extension being a common feature in certain letters when standing at the end of words in the Addition.

Now turning to Shakespeare's signature No. 3, we find in the two final letters *pe* exact replicas (1) of the initial *p* of the first two words quoted above—a short vertical stem commencing with a small hook or serif, a horizontal cross-bar, and a completing curve to form the head-loop; and (2) of the final *e* of the second word 'peace'—a letter of two disconnected concave curves, the upper one extending in a horizontal stroke because the letter stands at the end of the word.

This identity of letters in the formally written signature with letters in the formally written words in the Addition is a further important testimony in support of the contention that in the Addition we have indeed an example of Shakespeare's handwriting.

We can imagine the probable course in which Shakespeare's treatment of the scene developed and how it affected the character of his handwriting. In

---

[1] In fact the letter is constructed on the lines of the second capital P of the Addition, described below, p. 107.

the first page he had written enough to represent the surging tumult and wrangling of the mob; then, when he turned the leaf and began the second page, it was time to bring into active prominence the principal figure in the play. And thus he opened the second page with a few trivial exclamations. Then he pondered on the manner of More's coming addresses to the crowd—and, while he pondered, he wrote the three words which have been quoted, mechanically using his pen in slow movement and shaping his letters in set form, just as any of us might do while our thoughts are wandering to what should be written next. But with Shakespeare there was but little need for delay. He had barely scored down the three words, when his course was decided—and his pen at once became active again and he finished off the line with the fourth word, not in formal set letters but in ordinary cursive script. Thus he resumes and runs on in the rest of the second page with his composition, inscribing More's preliminary speeches in a style of writing gradually becoming less formally clerical than that of the first page, and beginning to develope the more deliberate character which, as already explained, finds full expression in the writing of the greater speech which fills most of the third page.

Besides resemblances in the shapes of individual letters, two personal usages show themselves both in Shakespeare's Signatures and in the Addition, which point to identity.

In the first place, at some time or other Shakespeare adopted the practice of writing an Italian long s ($\int$) as the second s in his surname. This letter is seen in three of the extant Signatures, Nos. 2, 3 and 6. In No. 1 the second s is entirely omitted in the abbreviated surname; and No. 4 is too much defaced for a decision on the form of the letter. In No. 5 alone (one of the signatures to the will) the English long f appears. This occurrence of the English letter is curious, for Shakespeare had only just subscribed the main signature (No. 6) to the will with the Italian letter. It may be attributed to a mental lapse—an involuntary resumption of a disused style. It proves, at least, that at some earlier period Shakespeare wrote his surname with the English long f. His adoption of the Italian letter was probably a mere matter of convenience, the foreign letter being more simple and handy than the native letter which would stand rather clumsily next to the tall letter *k*. The practice of mingling Italian and English letters was not uncommon in England in Shakespeare's day; but this *f* was the only letter of the Italian alphabet that he adopted in his signatures. It seems, then, more than a coincidence that the only Italian letter to be found in the lines of the Addition is the long *f*—which occurs in the word 'seriant' (l. 17, marg.) and is added in a minute size as a correction to the word 'warre' (l. 113)[1].

---

[1] In the transcript of the Addition, printed in *Shakespeare's Handwriting*, p. 95, I was led by the occurrence of a waving stroke, between lines 102 and 103, attached to the word 'only' in line 102, to read it as an Italian long *s* (*f*) interpolated possibly to convert 'only' into 'souly' (*solely*). I also read the third word in line 103 (deleted by a double horizontal stroke) as 'hys,' a pendent loop appearing to be the tail of the *y*. But some of my friends, experts in palæography, who have examined the passage in the MS. more closely than I have had the opportunity of doing, have given an opinion that the deleted word should be read 'his,' and that the loop which I had taken for the tail of a *y* is only part of a rambling scrawl with which the whole surface of the word is covered; and further, that the supposed

The second personal usage referred to is connected with the practice of attaching fine introductory up-strokes to certain letters when standing at the beginning of a word—a practice which seems to have been chiefly in vogue among expert calligraphers and professional scribes, but was also to some extent in more general use. The writing-books of the period show that these ornamental upstrokes were attachments to letters in writing the 'Secretary' hand, the ordinary current English hand of the time; and their presence in those books, which gave in their plates the different styles of handwriting practised by professional calligraphers and writing-masters, proves that upstrokes must have been a common feature in the copy-books of children at school. It is also in this connection an interesting fact that their employment in writing lessons persisted down to our own times, and that it ceased only when the copy-book passed away as an old-fashioned, but, for all that, a by no means useless, instrument of popular education.

As stated above, the principal signature, No. 6, to Shakespeare's will, written evidently with formality, is introduced by the words 'By me'; and the *m* of

Italian long *s* is nothing more than a pen-flourish finishing off the scrawl or one of the deleting strokes. However, it is not agreed how the scrawl is to be interpreted. A suggestion that it is intended for an ampersand (symbol for 'and') can hardly be accepted, as it bears no resemblance to the ampersand of the English hand of the period.

I venture to submit that, as it was the practice of the writer of the Addition to use a single stroke of the pen for deletion, while a double stroke is here employed, and as it would be futile to write an emendation in the tangle of a deleted word, the deletion and the scrawling are not the work of the author, but of some would-be corrector or correctors who have not been altogether successful in their endeavour.

'me' and the *W* of the Christian name are both
furnished with delicate upstrokes. Hence it may be
inferred that the employment of such ornaments was
a habit with Shakespeare—a habit which he would
have first acquired in his school-days—and that in
any written work from his hand there would be found
instances of this practice. Accordingly, in the lines
of the Addition we are not surprised to see frequent
upstrokes attached to one or other of the amenable
letters. Yet the mere occurrence of these upstrokes
in one of the Signatures and in the Addition is not in
itself to be taken as a proof that both documents come
from the hand of the same writer. It is not the use of
the upstrokes, but the style in which they are written
that is significant and suggests identity. Of the two
upstrokes in signature No. 6, while the first, attached
to the *m*, is of medium length, the second belonging to
the *W* is remarkable in being unusually long and in
leading off with a finely-drawn narrow opening which
resembles an elongated needle-eye, a formation so rare
that it suggests a personal peculiarity of the writer;
but, leaving the consideration of this latter upstroke
for the moment, it will be convenient to turn to the
Addition and survey the larger field of upstrokes
which it presents.

The upstrokes in the Addition are fairly numerous;
but their insertion does not appear to have been
governed by any rule, but rather to be due to the
passing mood or fancy of the writer. Planted pretty
closely in some lines; in others they are sparse. The
letters to which they may be attached are *i*, *m*, *n*,
twin-stemmed *r*, *v* and *w*, when any one of them is
the first letter of a word; but there are more or less
numerous instances of omission to attach the up-

strokes. The two letters of which there are the largest number of upstroked examples are *w* and *m*: the former letter is used in the total number of lines nearly 80 times, and only 25 of them are without the upstroke; and of *m*, out of more than 60 instances, not a third part are unprovided. On the other hand, out of some 40 examples of *n*, little more than a third part have the upstroke; and, of the more limited examples of *i*, *r*, and *v*, those with, and those without, upstrokes are practically equal.

Most of the upstrokes of the Addition are of a simple character, that is to say, they are delicately fine strokes carried up obliquely by a single action of the pen. But they vary in length: being in some instances short, more generally of medium measurement, and occasionally of exaggerated dimensions. This tendency to lengthen the upstrokes beyond normal limits has effected a change from the simple stroke. Unconsciously, no doubt, the writer began to feel the need of getting some support for the lengthening strokes, something to give an impetus to the extended upward motion of the pen; and accordingly we find this relief secured by the introduction of an auxiliary quick preliminary downstroke which, starting first, catches the upstroke, forms in conjunction with it a barb, right or left, as e.g. in 'is' (l. 62), 'moore' (l. 45), 'must' (l. 130), 'nor' (l. 136), 'rebell' (l. 114), 'unreverent' (l. 110), 'with' (l. 51), 'weele' (l. 142), and imparts the desired impetus. A further developement takes place when the auxiliary downstroke happens to fall on the very path to be occupied by the upstroke and is actually covered by it as the latter travels in upward course: a combination which is betrayed by the thickening or intensifying of the stroke, as in

PLATE V

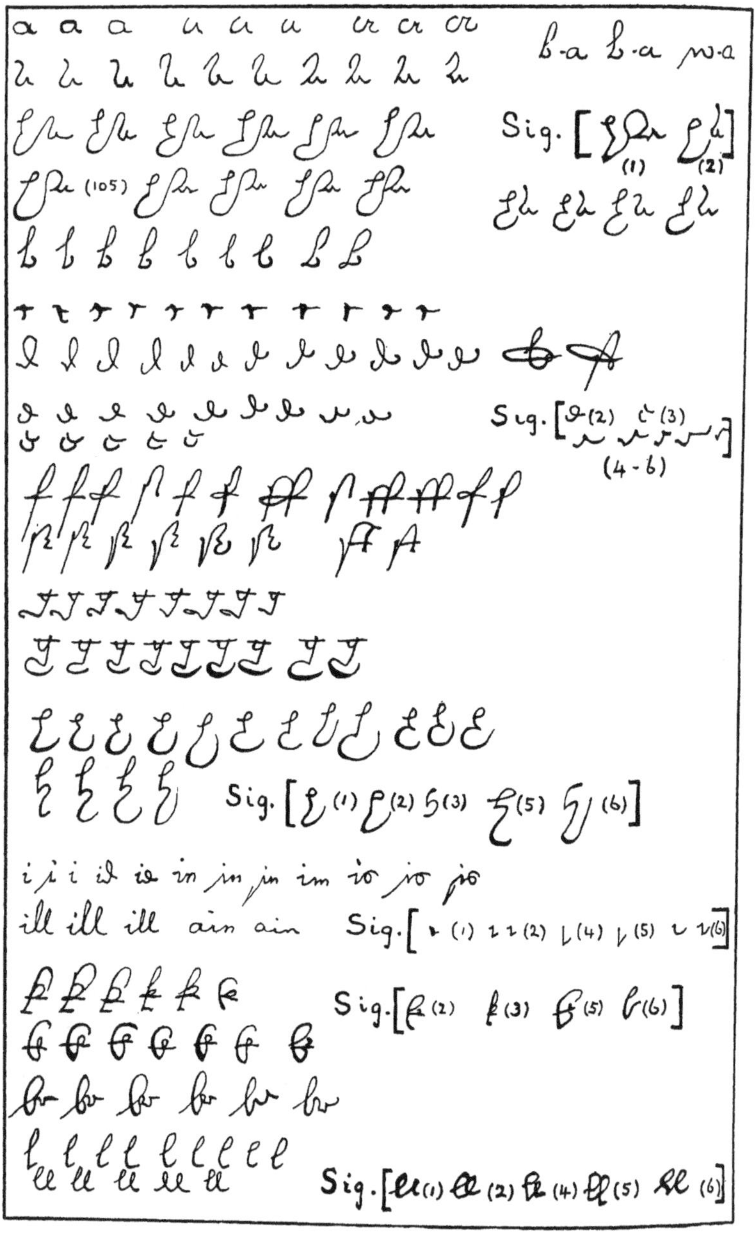

THE SMALL LETTERS OF THE SIGNATURES AND THE

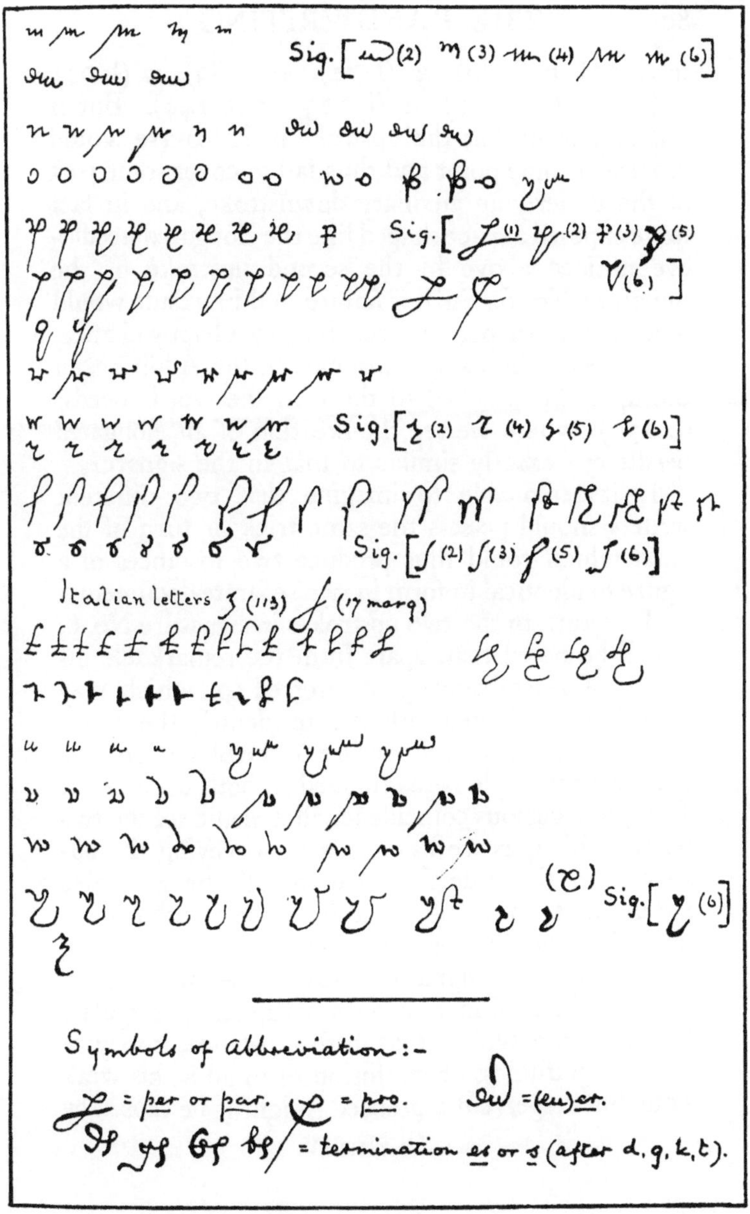

PLATE VI

Sig. [ᴟ (2) ᴟ (3) ᴟ (4) /ᴟ ᴟ (6)]

Sig. [ʃ (1) ʃ (2) ʃ (3) ʃ (5) ʃ (6)]

Sig. [ʒ (2) ʒ (4) ʒ (5) ʒ (6)]

Sig. [ʃ (2) ʃ (3) ʃ (5) ʃ (6)]

Italian letters ʒ (113) ʃ (17 marg)

Sig. [ʒ (6)]

Symbols of abbreviation :-

ꝑ = per or par.   ꝓ = pro.   ꝰ =(eu)er.

ꝡ ꝡ ꝡ ꝡ / = termination es or s (after d, g, k, t).

ADDITION (D) TO THE PLAY OF "SIR THOMAS MORE"

w (l. 55), *r* (l. 56), *w* (l. 74), *m* (l. 89), *m* (l. 90), *i* (l. 95), *w* (l. 108), *w* (l. 125), *n* (l. 144). But it might happen that the upstroke in its course would deviate at some point and thus fail to cover some part of the underlying auxiliary downstroke, and in fact leave exposed a space shaped like the elongated needle-eye noticed above in the second upstroke of the signature No. 6. Such a failure and its result would indeed be a rare occurrence. But, by a happy chance, it does occur in a single instance in the Addition, in the upstroke attached to the *n* in the word 'needs' (l. 130)[1] where we see the creation of an elongated needle-eye exactly similar to that in the signature.

Is it reasonable to imagine that two different writers should possess the same trick or turn of the hand which could thus produce two instances of a figure so identical in form in two separate documents?

To return to the two upstrokes in signature No. 6, it will be noted that, apart from the remarkable instance of resemblance just referred to, which may indeed be considered sufficient to identify the writer of the Addition with the writer of the Signatures, the same delicate style is maintained in both documents. It is also a curious coincidence that *m* and *w*, the two letters which, as we have seen in surveying the upstrokes in the Addition, are, of all the amenable letters, those most subject to have the attachment of upstrokes, should happen to be the two letters carrying upstrokes in that signature. Of course the use of an upstroke in conjunction with a capital is irregular; but it is quite evident that in this instance, it may be from forgetfulness or confusion of mind in his weak state, Shakespeare did proceed (might it be caused by

[1] See Plate IV.

a subconscious association in his thoughts of *m* and *w* as the two letters most subject to the upstroke?) to inscribe an upstroke to accompany the capital *W* of his Christian name. The long oblique stroke is carried up far above the line of writing and stands in the air, as if in expectation of a capital letter; but the capital *W* has to be united with it at a lower level, as if the writer suddenly found that he must ignore the portion of the upstroke extending overhead, in order to form the capital on the usual lines of that letter.

Analysis of the alphabets of the Signatures and the Addition

[In the following analysis of the individual letters, both small letters and capitals, which are found in Shakespeare's Signatures and in the Addition (D) to the play of *Sir Thomas More*, it is to be noted that the Addition takes precedence in the descriptions, as being the more important document, both for actual extent and for palæographical value; the Signatures on the other hand affording far slighter material for analysis. But, at the same time, whenever reference is made in the general descriptions to any feature in the Signatures, care has been taken to state clearly its provenance; and further, in order to guard against ambiguity, all notes and remarks which concern the Signatures alone are enclosed within square brackets.

I have also found it convenient to coin two words, viz. 'pre-link' and 'post-link'; the first to define the linking of a letter with a foregoing letter, the other its linking with a following letter.

Letters of the English 'Secretary' hand (both small and capital), which do not occur either in the Addition or in the Signatures, are given in the Plates, for convenience of reference. They are enclosed in curved brackets.

With regard to the drawings of letters which occupy

Plates V–VII, it has not been possible, with the limited space at disposal, to do much more than to present them in skeleton-outline. But it is hoped that this will be sufficient to illustrate the construction of the individual letters.]

i. *The Small Letters*

Letter a. The letter *a* appears in the Addition in several forms, which may be arranged in two groups. The first is the group of the normal closed letter; the second is the group of the normal open letter.

The normal closed letter is the scrivener's letter of the period, which differs but little from the letter in our modern English cursive hand. As a rule, it is here neatly formed and of a broad type. In rapid or careless writing, however, there is a natural tendency to leave the ring of the letter more or less open at the top, when it may be mistaken for a *u*; but this imperfect form must not be regarded as anything more than an accidental variety of the closed letter. There is also in the Addition another variety, the origin of which may likewise be ascribed to rapid writing. It is a disjointed letter in which the ring and the minim, instead of being written in close conjunction, stand apart and are only held together by a top link (as in the modern German cursive letter), the ring being not always perfectly closed. Thus written, the letter may be mistaken for *œ* or *oi* (see Plate IV, ll. 130, 131, 133). The gradual developement of this dislocation of the normal closed letter may be followed in its stages in the documents of the time. But in a final shape it is not often found; and therefore its occurrence as a finished and uniform letter in the Addition (where it appears some two dozen times, chiefly in the first page where the writing is in the scrivener style) would suggest the inference that the writer had learned its use, as an alternative variety of the normal closed letter, in the course of education.

It is to be noticed that there occur (ll. 92, 93) two abnormal *a*'s (each as the indefinite article), formed like the disjointed letter just described, but also having a hooked forelimb which is one of the special features of the second group. This composite letter is found nowhere else and may be a freak of carelessness.

The normal open letter and its varieties which constitute the second group are more elaborate in construction. The primary letter is open at the top, like *u*, and in this respect its form does not vary. Attached, as a kind of forelimb, to its first minim is a tall vertical or slanting stroke, inclining to concave curvature and either clubbed or thickened at the top, or furnished with a preliminary bow or hook on the left side. The clubbed forelimb usually merges at once with the first minim; the hooked forelimb either merges in the same way, or, more frequently, is carried obliquely and independently towards, or quite down to, the base-line of writing, and the two minims of the open letter are added to its under-side, the butt-end of the forelimb, generally finished in a fine point, being left uncovered. If, however, the forelimb is inclined to curvature, the butt-end may assume a different shape, as will presently be explained.

The existence of the forelimb, which is a conspicuous feature in the construction of the letter in many examples of the English hand of the Elizabethan period, and which can be traced back to earlier times, seems to have invited the practice, which occurs in some hands, as it does in the Addition before us, of linking certain letters with the open *a* by means of an overhead arched link which incorporates the forelimb. Such linkings are *ha, ma, na, pa, sa, ua,* the most frequent being *ha*; but, before noticing them, it will be of advantage first to examine the instance which occurs in Shakespeare's signature, No. 1. For the handwriting of this signature is on a larger scale than that of the Addition and therefore affords a favourable opportunity for more clearly explaining the construction of the open *a* as modified by being linked with the preceding *h.*

[In the Signatures of Shakespeare the closed *a* (not always perfectly formed) is used, except in Nos. 1 and 2. In the surname of No. 1 the *a* is the open *u*-shaped letter. It is connected with the preceding *h* by means of an overhead arched link proceeding from the underline pendent bow of that letter. Its construction is as follows. The pen, instead of breaking off when it had completed the finishing stroke of the pendent bow, continues to carry it upwards, and arriving at the base-line of writing proceeds to describe a figure resembling a rather irregular circle on a larger scale than that of the body of the letter: first swerving to the left, to gain room, it describes the left-hand half of the circumference; then, having reached the crown of the arch where the link may be said to have discharged its proper function, it proceeds to describe the right-hand half of the circumference, into which it first incorporates the concave forelimb of the open *a* and thus forms the back of the letter in course of construction; next, having now been brought down close to the base-line of writing, the pen moves horizontally to the left and forms a pointed projection, or spur, from the lower end of the back of the letter, and would thus complete the full circle but for a minute space left unoccupied between the point of the spur and the up-risen link; then the pen, without being lifted, moves to the right along the line of the spur, and at its root adds the first minim of the open *a* and then the second, both minims being rather negligently formed and sloping backward. It is important to note that it is the sustained curving action of the hand in the developement of the circle that provides room for the creation of the spur.]

To return to the Addition: the best example therein of the linking of *ha* just described occurs in the word 'that' in l. 105. After making allowance for the smaller scale of writing, it will be seen that the formation of the open letter *a*, accompanied with its spur, is exactly the same as that of the corresponding letter in the Shakespearian signature. Other instances are to be found, but more hurriedly written, as e.g. 'has' (l. 12), 'hath' (l. 102), 'that' (ll. 117, 135), 'harber' (l. 127). The tendency to the curving action, which seems inherent in this hand, has the effect in many instances, both when the open *a* is linked with other letters mentioned above as well as with *h*, and also even when it is written independently, of lengthening the exposed pointed butt-end of the fore-limb in the direction of spur-formation, but in no instance so decisively as in the linking with *h*.

To conclude these remarks upon the arched linkings of the open *a* with other letters, it is to be borne in mind that such linkings are not uniformly made use of. The pairs of letters for the most part are also subject to linking in the ordinary way with the common links which may unite any couples of letters. There are also many instances in which *h* with its pendent underline bow and open *a* with its standard forelimb come together and seem made to invite each other to join by means of the overhead arched link, yet curiously remain independent; the pendent bow hangs in suspense under the line and the unbending forelimb is left in the air.

[An instance of this standing apart of the two letters is to be seen in Shakespeare's Signature No. 2. The pendent bow of the *h* is curved upwards but stops short just when it reaches the base-line of the writing, and the forelimb of the open *a*, clubbed at the head and curved, merges directly with the first minim of the letter[1].]

The two forms (closed and open) of the *a* of the two groups are used indifferently in the Addition; but the open letter with the forelimb is generally preferred, and it is used more frequently than the simple letter at the beginning of words or when it stands alone as the indefinite article[2].

It is noticeable that the writer of the Addition

---

[1] In *Shakespeare's Handwriting* I incorrectly stated that the two letters were linked, but that the ink had partially failed to mark the full course of the link in the extension upwards of the pendent bow of the *h* to join the forelimb of the *a*.

[2] In connection with the history of the forelimb of the open *a* group, there is a curious and interesting instance of its transmutation, through oblivion of origin, into a conventional symbol. It occurs in the Audit Office Revels MS. containing a list of the plays acted before Charles I and his Queen in 1636–7, from which a facsimile is given in Mr Ernest Law's *More about Shakespeare 'Forgeries,'* 1913, p. 59. Here the scribe, using the ordinary *a*, marks it in almost all instances with an emphatic acute accent, which can be nothing but a survival of the obsolete forelimb.

generally observes a rule not to link a letter, which does not naturally pre-link, such as closed *a*, to a letter which does not naturally post-link, such as *b, o, v, w* (which turn-in the final curve and thus present no point of connection). But in a very few cases, when closed *a* follows one of those letters, it is provided with a very minute hyphen too small to be of practical use: perhaps a lingering reminiscence of early schooling.

Letter b. The main stem of this letter is normally provided with a well-defined initial loop, which however is not always closed and may thus become an open bow. The main stroke should be carried down direct to the base-line of writing and there form a characteristic sharp point at the base of the letter, whence the finishing curve starts; but in rapid and careless writing this sharp base-point is lost by the rounding of the base, as in our modern letter. That this base-point was an essential feature in the true formation of the letter is shown by an instance of the letter written swiftly and loosely, in which the point is even looped (l. 146). The base-curve is finished off by being turned in towards the main stem, thus causing the letter to be not post-linkable. If a link should occur, it is to be regarded as belonging to the following letter.

Letter c. The letter *c* is formed by two independent strokes: the first vertical; the second horizontal. The vertical should be slightly curved or hollow-backed, sometimes beginning with a short head upstroke or serif, and being at first firmly impressed but then gradually fining off to a point. The curve is fairly well maintained in the more rapid and lighter hand of the scrivener style; but in the more deliberate hand of the latter part of the Addition it is straightened and is more heavily impressed. The horizontal is a finer stroke, proceeding from the top or from near the top of the vertical, and is generally of moderate length, except occasionally when the letter stands at the end of a word. In a few instances an abnormal foot is added at right angles to the base of the vertical.

The letter pre-links at the top of the vertical; it post-links by means of the horizontal.

Letter d. This letter is always in the round, looped form; and the loop is almost invariably clearly written —only rarely, when in reduced size, is it blind. The letter is usually fairly upright; but when it follows a tall letter, such as *l* or long *s*, the loop is generally bent back in a more horizontal position and is lengthened; not however after double *l*. At the end of a word the letter is often finished off with a flourish dotted at the end. This letter, when diminished in size, and looped *e* when written large, are very much alike and may easily be confused and induce misreadings.

Letter e. This letter is in two forms. The first, which is the ordinary form, is the more cursive looped letter—the loop reversed. The loop is usually clearly written, but at the end of a word, and written hurriedly, it is sometimes blind or slurred. Like *d*, it often ends in a flourish and dot. Final *e* after *k* (as in 'like') is often negligently formed, the loop being blind or slurred and flourished. The likeness between *d* and looped *e* and their possible confusion have been noticed above: see the two words at the end of lines 78, 79 (Plate III), 'braule' and 'clothd,' in which the final letters *e* and *d* may be declared identical.

The second shape of *e* is a more formal letter composed of two concave curves, disconnected: it is in fact only a less cursive variety of the looped letter, the connection between the curves being omitted. It is employed only occasionally in the Addition. It should be noted that, like the looped letter, this form of *e* pre-links with the lower curve, and post-links with the upper curve, the lower curve being written before the upper one.

[In the Signatures, the ordinary reverse-looped letter appears in No. 2, the loop large and clear; in No. 3, the second shape, composed of two separate concave curves. In the will-signatures the ordinary letter is used, but the loop is slurred and becomes a mere tick.]

Letter f. This letter varies in different parts of the Addition, but it may generally be described as of two forms: the lighter form which is prevalent in the scrivener style of writing, and the heavier form which is more general in the deliberately written lines.

The construction of the letter of the first form, which is a long-shafted letter, is as follows: the full length of the thin straight shaft is first written, commencing well above the line of writing and descending far below it and ending in a fine-drawn point; to this the head-curve is added and is then either drawn down and inward, like the lash of a driving-whip, so as to traverse the shaft, and the horizontal cross-bar is then made—all in one action of the pen; or, if the letter stands at the end of a word (the word 'of' being the most common instance), the lash is left hanging loose and the cross-bar is omitted. In the ordinary handwriting of the time, the lash of final *f* is made to hang clear away from the shaft and is slightly clubbed or thickened at the end. In this Addition it is finished off with a flourish shaped like a left-shouldered ᵹ. The junction of the head-curve with the top of the shaft is not always accurately closed.

The second, heavier, form of the letter has a thickened and generally shortened shaft made by drawing a descending stroke which starts from the line of writing, and then carrying the pen up again on the same stroke and thus doubling it in bulk (sometimes carelessly looping it); next, without lifting the pen, forming the upper half of the shaft, above the line, and the head-curve; and lastly finishing off the letter in the way described above, either with a cross-bar, or, in the case of a final *f*, without it.

When the letter is doubled, the down-drawn stroke of the head-curve of the first letter (which I have compared to a whip-lash) is not drawn in to the shaft, but is carried on to the descending shaft of the second letter, which is then completed in the usual way, the head-curve of the second letter out-topping that of the first letter; and the lash of this second letter is then drawn back to traverse the shafts of both letters, and then the cross-bar for both letters is made in a single finishing stroke—all by one action of the pen.

Occasionally, from failure of accuracy in the stroke, the cross-bar gets twisted into a loop. In the case of linked *ft*, the head-curve of the *f* merging with the shaft of the *t*, a long independent cross-bar is added, to serve both letters.

Letter g. The letter *g* appears in two styles, distinguished by the different methods of finishing off the tail of the letter. The construction of the head of the letter is uniform: a *v*-shaped semicircle is first written, the right-hand horn often projecting slightly above the level of the other, and the pen then makes a descending stroke to form the stem which, in the one style of the letter, is carried down to a sufficient length and is then bent back at a sharp angle, the line being now more or less curved and being finished off with a clubbing or thickening or minute curl; or, in the other style, the finishing stroke is turned round again to the right and ends in a broad curved stroke resembling an inverted scythe-blade. The head of the letter should be normally closed with a horizontal line; but complete closure is sometimes carelessly neglected. The first style of the letter is more common in the earlier and more cursively written portion of the Addition; the second style is more prevalent in the more deliberately written lines. The variety of ways in which the descending limb of letter *g* is treated in examples of the English 'Secretary' hand of this period may justify us in regarding it as a letter in which we might specially find, from its style, a clue to the identity of the writer.

The letter pre-links by means of the left horn of the *v*-shaped head; it post-links by the horizontal head-line.

Letter h. The letter *h* is the most sinuous letter in the Elizabethan cursive alphabet[1], and invites a great variety of manipulation without essentially altering its character. The letter normally commences with a head-loop which usually stands well above the line of writing, but tends, in the course of hurried writing and especially when pre-linked, to sink more nearly to the level of the letters in the line. The shaft is then

[1] In *Ant. and Cleop.* IV. vii. 7, Scarus exclaims: 'I had a wound here that was like a T, But now 'tis made an H.' This is unintelligible as it is printed; but substitute for the capitals T and H the old English cursive minuscules *t* (a straight-cut letter) and *h* (a sinuous letter like a mangled wound), and the meaning is clear.

carried down below the base level, and thence bending to the left it describes a pendent bow below the line, and either ends there, or is carried upwards for the purpose of post-linking. Occasionally a modified form of the normal letter is used in which the shaft is carried down to the base-line, and thence, as in our modern cursive letter, springs the arch of the body of the letter, from which the pendent bow descends. [The *h* in Shakespeare's signatures Nos. 1 and 2 is normal; in Nos. 5 and 6 it is of this modified form; in No. 3 it is an uncursive letter, the signature being purposely written in formal characters (see p. 60).] In other and more frequent instances the letter, by curving the stem and then throwing off the pendent bow at a sharp angle, assumes a shape not unlike italic ε.

The letter pre-links naturally by its head-loop; it post-links by its pendent bow, either in the ordinary way by linking in the line of writing, or, if the following letter is open *a*, by means of an arched curve carried above the line in prolongation of the pendent bow (see the description of Letter *a*, above). [The letters *ha* in signature No. 1 are linked in this manner.]

Letter i. This letter plays a rather insignificant part in the alphabet of the Addition; but it has a certain interest for the purpose of the present enquiry. In no position is it a conspicuous letter. At the beginning of a word it is no more than of normal size; in the middle of a word it is often reduced, in hurried writing, to a very small scale. The letter is generally dotted.

But the writer is inclined to vary the shape of the letter by altering, under certain conditions, the normal curved base into a pointed base, the change being governed by the character of the link connecting the *i* with the next following letter. If the link is a rising link, requiring the pen to move upwards, the writer in anticipation hastens to begin that movement and so makes the base pointed. Otherwise the base should normally be a round curve. This appears to be the general rule; but it is to be noted that it is not consistently observed.

The letter *i* is one of the letters to which the ornamental initial upstroke can be attached.

[The letter appears with both the normal curved base and the pointed base in the Signatures which have the Christian name more or less extended. In No. 6 the first *i* linked with the double *l* has correctly the curved base, while the letter linked to the *a* is pointed. In the weakly written No. 2, while the second *i* is likewise pointed, the first, which should be curved at the base, is also rather pointed. The Christian name in No. 1 is too much huddled for consideration; and in Nos. 4 and 5 the exaggerated point given to the *i* is rather to be attributed to spasmodic uncontrolled effort. All that can be fairly said in this particular is that, as in the Addition, so in the Signatures, both curved and pointed bases appear.]

Letter k. This is a letter of various forms: (1) the normal scrivener's letter, having a top-curved or looped stem, with a horizontal base-stroke, or more frequently a foot at right angles to the stem, and a central loop and cross-bar attached to the middle of the stem. This form is sometimes imperfectly or clumsily written when it post-links with *e*; and in one instance it is hurriedly written without a foot (l. 102); (2) a more cursive form; the stem curved at the top and itself inclined to curvature; the base round (as in our modern cursive *l*) and carried up to the middle level where a small twisted loop (often blind) is described; the pen then moving horizontally to the left, to reach the stem, and then to the right, thus making the cross-bar; (3) a rare form, like No. 2, but omitting the small twisted loop, which however is represented by a heavy comma added in its place; (4) the same *l*-formation, but the end of the base-curve terminating in a minute bow (sometimes blind), the letter being thus completed without a cross-bar. This form is used chiefly in words ending in *ke*, as 'lyke,' 'shake,' the linked *e* being negligently written with the loop blind and flourished.

[In the Signatures, the *k* of No. 1 is defaced by a blot; in No. 2 (not well formed) and in No. 3, it is of the normal scrivener's type (1); in No. 5, it is apparently of the rare (3) type with a dot representing the middle loop; and in No. 6 it appears to be of the (4) type, without a cross-bar.]

Letter l. This is usually a round-backed letter; the stem looped, generally with a well-defined loop. In the same manner as that already noticed in the case of letter *i*, there is a tendency to sharpen the base curve. When the *l* is doubled, the two letters are often written on a small scale and the second rather tends to be smaller than the first, and, in consequence of the quick-curving action of the hand, they are drawn out of their correct slope and may thus offer occasion for misreading: e.g. 'rule' might be mis-read 'ride.'

[Some of these characteristics are to be noticed in the double *l* of the Signatures.]

Letter m. This letter is never very well formed by

the impatient writer of the Addition, and inclines to angularity. When it stands at or near the beginning of a word, the correct convexity (though angular) of its minims is usually maintained. It often runs small in the middle of a word; and when written in connection with *n* or *u* and other letters of similar formation it inclines to concavity, and from haste it is not always provided with the correct number of minims. Final *m* sometimes ends with a slightly lengthened straight minim, not turned up; on the other hand it is also sometimes concave and turned up at the end, especially in the word 'them,' no doubt owing to the curving impetus given to the hand by the preceding *e*. The letters *m* and *n* are among the letters to which the ornamental initial upstroke can be attached.

[In the Signatures may be noticed the impatiently huddled letter in No. 1; the *m* turned up in a flourish in No. 2; and the small tremulous letter with an accidental final tag in No. 3. The *m* of 'me' in No. 6 has the initial ornamental upstroke.]

Letter n. This letter generally follows the example of *m*. Final *n*, especially when following *e*, tends to be distinctly concave and turns up with a flourish, as in the word 'men.'

Letter o. This is a self-contained letter. In construction, the circle commences on the left side of the circumference, the joint not being always perfectly closed, the end of the ring even sometimes overlapping the commencement. As an extreme instance, in the word 'woold,' l. 125, the two *o*'s resemble two inverted *c*'s. But generally the letter is well-formed and is scarcely ever blind or blotted, and the circle is fairly perfect. By its construction therefore it is neither a pre-linking nor a post-linking letter, although in practice it is linked up by preceding letters, except the non-post-linking letters *b*, *v*, *w*; but in such cases the link belongs to the preceding letter. Instances of unlinked words occur, as 'o bay,' 'woold.' Occasionally (as in the case of *a*, noticed above) a minute hyphen stands between *o* and a non-post-linking letter, such as *w*, or between two *o*'s (e.g. 'w-oold,' 'sho-old'); but, as this only rarely occurs, the presence of the hyphen may be an accidental survival of a former, but discontinued, habit of the writer, dating from school-days.

In the words 'you' and 'your,' written 'yo^u' and 'yor,' the *o* is left open at the top and is linked with the letter above the line. When following *f*, the letter *o* is sometimes jammed up close to the *f*, making a kind of monogram of the two letters. This treatment of the letter, especially in short words, is noticeable in Elizabethan handwriting.

Letter p. This letter appears in various shapes, but they may be grouped generally in two classes. The first is nearest to the normal scrivener's letter: the head has a fore-limb, shaped like the figure 2, with which the head-loop is combined and then continues with a stem or descender of varying length, rarely long and pointed, but usually short or very short and curved and carried up in order to post-link. The second class, which is in common use, has a simple loop-head, the short initial oblique stroke being slightly waved by pressure of the hand; the descender carried down to some length, sometimes to great length, often being a long dashing stroke ending in a point or being returned to the line of writing by a post-linking upstroke.

[In the Signatures the *p* of No. 2 is of the first class, with a straight stem post-linking by an up-stroke; that of Nos. 5 and 6, of the second class.]

There are also a few abnormal letters, one of which may be noticed. It is a short, truncated, deliberately written letter, resembling very nearly a printer's ordinary lower-case letter p, and having a short vertical stem commencing with a small hook or serif on the left; then a short horizontal cross-bar is drawn to form the base of the head-loop, which is completed by the addition of the necessary curve. [The letter *p* in signature No. 3 which is written in deliberately formed letters, is of this type (see above, p. 73).]

The shape of the letter *p* which is used in the symbols for *par* or *per*, and for *pro*, is that described here under the second class. [The *p*, with cross-stroke through the stem, in signature No. 1, belongs to this variety; the method of crossing the stem is the same as that followed in the construction of the symbol for *par* or *per* in the Addition.]

Letter q. There are, in the Addition, only four instances of the use of this letter; in one of them the ring is open at the top. The letter calls for no other remark, being practically of the same form as that of our modern cursive letter.

Letter r. The normal twin-stemmed English letter, composed of two short vertical strokes connected at the base by a more or less arched curve, and termi-nating at the top of the last limb with a shoulder by means of which the letter post-links, is in general use. It is very uniform in character, except for the natural fluctuations of the hand. The connecting base-arch is sometimes exaggerated and rises too high;

the two verticals are sometimes brought too closely together; and in post-linking there is a tendency to slur the shoulder and merge the final limb, the letter thus resembling a lower-case *n*. This is one of the letters to which the ornamental initial upstroke can be attached.

The left-shouldered ƺ occurs here and there, chiefly in the first page of the Addition, where the writing is more of the scrivener style. This letter is always used in the abbreviated word 'yoͬ' (*your*). [In the Signatures it is always left-shouldered.]

Letter s. There are two forms of this letter: the long ſ, employed, both single and doubled, at the beginning or in the middle of a word; and the small, round, looped letter used at the end of a word. The construction of the long ſ follows exactly that of the letter *f* already described, of course omitting the cross-bar of the latter. In the first page of the Addition, and in the second page in a less degree, the form prevails which is written with a lighter hand and which produces the shaft, in full length, from above to below the line of writing in a long pointed stroke. The head-curve is added to the shaft by a separate action of the pen, but in the hurry of writing the point of junction is not in all cases accurately closed. The head-curve, like the lash of a driving-whip, is brought down to the line of writing and there either post-links, or, if such post-linking is not permissible, it is drawn back to the shaft.

As in the case of *f*, a second heavier variety of long ſ is also employed and prevails in the third page, and to some extent appears also in the second page. In this variety a thickened and generally shorter shaft is made by drawing a descending stroke from the line of writing, and then carrying the pen up again on the same stroke, thus doubling it in bulk, and then, without lifting the pen, forming the head-curve and post-linking it, or drawing it in to the shaft, as already described.

When the letter is doubled, the head-curve of the first f is carried on to, and is incorporated with, the descender of the second f, which is then completed as if a single letter, the head-curve of the second letter out-topping that of the first letter—the whole process being accomplished without lifting the pen.

Long f post-links, by its head-curve, with certain letters; not with others. For example, it post-links with *t*, not with *c*; perhaps to avoid ambiguity.

The small circular *s*, used at the end of a word, is generally a fairly symmetrical round loop, the loose end of which is left, in the air, at the top of the letter, hanging to the right or turned back in a curve.

A long *f* of the Italian type appears in the correction of a word, l. 113; and a letter of the same type, looped at the lower end, is in 'seriant,' l. 17 margin.

[Shakespeare uses in most of the Signatures an Italian long *f* as the medial *s* of the surname, inscribed with a slender stroke as if with the point of the pen turned inwards. It appears in Nos. 2, 3 and 6. It is the only Italian letter thus employed. In No. 5 he writes the English letter.]

Letter t. There is much variety in the forms in which this letter is written in the Addition; but they may generally be grouped in two main classes, the first following the normal type of the letter of the scriveners, with variations; the second a simpler type, also with variations. Both classes are used throughout the Addition; but the first prevails in the first two pages, the second in the third page.

The more carefully formed letter of the first class
has a swaying stem, curved at the top, with a horizontal foot at the base, either extending both right
and left of the stem, or only to the right; the cross-bar
cutting the stem low down, or extending to the right.
The top-curve of the stem may become looped, especially when linked. A less elaborate form of this class
has the top-curve, but discards the foot, and its cross-bar
is represented by an arm projecting to the right from
near the base of the stem. This form is used very
commonly linked with *h* in words beginning with *th*,
and is usually written with a light hand. In rapid writing, a loop is sometimes made at the base of the stem.

The general type of the second class is a straight
heavy stem with an arm, representing the cross-bar,
projecting to the right from the stem, low down or
even from its very base. This style of letter is roughly
and forcibly inscribed and wants the finish of the
letters of the scrivener's type. In careless writing it
is often imperfectly or negligently written; and it also
takes a looped shape, which might be mistaken for
b or *l*. It is often written as a thick, stunted letter.

The cross-bar of *t*, when that letter is pre-linked
with *f* or long *f*, is very prominent.

Letter u. The letter *u* (represented by *v* at the
beginning of a word) is written in correct concave
formation; whereas, in the cases of *m* and *n*, it has
been shown that those letters, when written quickly,
tend to lose their proper convexity and to lapse into
concavity in the middle of a word—the action of the
writer's hand in the Addition being of the downward
not the rising, curve. Like *m* and *n* it is often
written negligently small. It was the custom of the
time to write the *u* of the word 'you' above the line,

as if the word were abbreviated; this final *u* tends to be flourished: in a few instances it stands, not above, but in, the line of writing.

Letter v. This letter is normally formed, and shows little variation. In the early part of the Addition the initial curve is in some instances written with a larger, sweeping stroke. In the deliberate hand, the heavy initial limb is to be noticed. The base-curve, being turned inwards, offers no facility for post-linking. To this letter and to *w* the ornamental initial up-stroke can be attached.

Letter w. What has been said of *v* applies equally to this letter, which in fact is constructed on the same lines, with an added initial minim. Like *v*, the initial curve is in some instances, in the earlier pages of the Addition, enlarged with a sweeping stroke; and, like *v*, this letter does not post-link. In the more deliberate hand of the third page the letter is of a heavier and more roughly formed type.

Letter x. No instance of this letter occurs.

Letter y. The normal form of this letter is written in a single action of the pen. At the foot of the initial stroke of the hand a small upward curve or fold is described, and thence descends the sweeping bow under the line, which may be carried up as a means of post-linking in the line, or, like the descending bow of *h*, it may be lifted in an arch above the line. In more hurried writing the small fold in the head is neglected, and the letter then differs but little from our modern cursive letter. A reduced form of the letter is used occasionally, which is kept almost within the limits of the letters in the line of writing; it nearly resembles a left-shouldered ȝ; and it might be mistaken for that letter.

Final *y* at the end of a word or line is often conspicuously flourished.

[A normal *y* occurs in Signature No. 6, in the introductory word 'By.']

Letter z. There is only one instance of this letter, l. 9. It is of normal type.

Abbreviations, etc.

In the Addition there are a few abbreviations of an ordinary character (Plate VI). They are:

Omission of final *n*, indicated by a horizontal stroke above the penultimate letter, as in *vppon* (ll. 19, 61).

Matie, a shortened form of 'majestie,' occurring thrice (ll. 73, 101, 121). There should be a horizontal stroke above the word, indicating contraction; but in two instances it is omitted, and in the third (l. 101) it is added carelessly, perhaps by a second hand. This is the usual contracted form of the word in use for a Sovereign's royal title. In the general sense of the word, we should rather have expected it to be written uncontracted.

The letter *p* with the stem looped and crossed horizontally, the symbol for the syllable *par* or *per*.

The letter *p* with a curve drawn from the left side and crossing the stem, the symbol for the syllable *pro.*

A curve or hook rising vertically above the line, a symbol for the syllable *er*, as in the word *ever* (l. 21).

A loop, in the line of writing, at the end of a word, a symbol indicating omission generally of final *es*, sometimes of *s*. In most instances this symbol appears in a rather ornamental shape, not unlike a modern cursive *s*, for which it might carelessly be mistaken.

PLATE VII

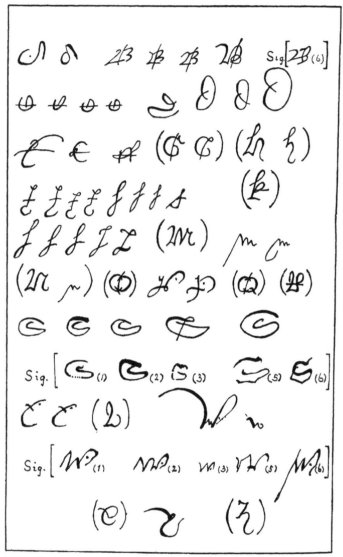

THE CAPITAL LETTERS OF THE SIGNATURES AND THE
ADDITION (D) TO THE PLAY OF "SIR THOMAS MORE"

All the above symbols were in common use, even into the eighteenth century.

[The abbreviations in Shakespeare's Signatures have already been explained.]

ii. *The Capital Letters*

The three pages of the Addition to the play of *Sir Thomas More* together with Shakespeare's six Signatures do not afford sufficient material to yield a complete alphabet of the capital letters which we may conjecture were made use of by Shakespeare (assuming that I am right in my contention that the Addition, as well as the Signatures, is in his autograph). But it fortunately happens that the majority of the letters are represented, namely, *A, B, C, D, E, ff (F), I (J), L, P, S, T, W, Y*, that is, thirteen out of the twenty-four. Thus eleven, namely, *G, H, K, M, N, O, Q, R, (U) V, X, Z*, are wanting; but this number may be further reduced if certain modifications are to be admitted, as will presently be shown.

The task, then, before us is not only to analyse the forms of the letters of which we can produce examples, but also to conjecture the character of the letters which are wanting. In the solution of the latter part of the enquiry we are assisted by the fact that Shakespeare wrote the native English hand, that he did not write the imported Italian hand. The only trace of foreign influence, as we have seen, is in his adoption of the Italian minuscule *f* in his Signatures. He would not therefore, like many writers of his time, have been tempted to mingle Italian forms with his English letters, thus composing a nondescript alphabet. The capital letters in his Signatures are of the English type; so too are the capitals of which we find examples in the Addition.

An interesting point is also to be noticed in the treatment of the capitals, namely, the facility with which the delicate curves of such letters as E (Addition, ll. 24, 30, 31); S (Addition, ll. 24, 25, &c.) and [Signature No. 1]; and T (Addition, ll. 30, 55) are accomplished. Shakespeare could hardly have claimed to be a fine calligrapher, although a fluent writer in the unrestrained scrivener style; but the larger scale of the capital letters no doubt afforded him scope for free play with his pen, and in the execution of the curves referred to he shows unusual dexterity. His hand, as a young man, was evidently naturally firm. If we are to place the date of the Addition in the year 1593–4, it would have been written in about his thirtieth year. He had then still in front of him some twenty years of strenuous dramatic composition and of actual hard manual labour with the pen before his hand was to show signs of the weakness which, as already described, is to be detected in his Signatures.

We first examine Shakespeare's extant capital letters:

Letter A. An instance of the scrivener's formal letter occurs in l. 43. It commences with an exaggerated base-curve, which is ornamented with a central dot; the body of the letter being an open angle without cross-bar. A rather simpler form, without the ornamental dot, is seen in l. 59.

Letter B. There are two forms of this elaborate letter in the Addition. The first, of which there are five instances (ll. 3, 37, 43, 59 and 89 margin), is constructed by three separate actions of the pen: (1) a fore-limb, shaped like a plough-share or a man-of-war's ram, the pen commencing with a small curve or hook and then moving obliquely to the point of the ram and thence horizontally to the right to a sufficient length to form the base-line of the letter; (2) the top horizontal line is then drawn, and the pen descending describes the two great bows, and should then make a junction with the extreme end of the base-line; (3) an obliquely vertical stroke, inclining to curvature, traverses the body of the letter and represents the main stem of the *B*. The junction of the lower bow with the end of the base-line is not always accurately adjusted.

[The capital *B* written by Shakespeare at the head of the words 'By me' prefixed to Signature No. 6 is constructed on the same lines as the letter in the Addition just described; but, owing to his infirmity, it is malformed, and the base-line rises too high.]

The second form of the letter in the Addition occurs in the margin of l. 70. It commences, like the other, with a fore-limb, but of a different pattern: a curved bold stroke descending to the base, where the pen adds a short connecting base-curve, and then rises in a bold sweep to form the body of the letter with its two great bows, all in one action. Then the obliquely vertical stroke, representing the main-stem of the *B*, is separately added.

Letter C. A formal letter of unpretentious type, written monotonously without much variation: a circular spiral letter in reverse action, like a modern cursive capital *O* loosely written; bisected by a horizontal cross-bar—this cross-bar and the initial curve being in fact the actual letter, and the finishing curve a flourish. It is to be noted that in the portion of the Addition written in scrivener style the capital *C* is used at the beginning of words, without regard to their position in the sentence, in preference to the minuscule letter. On the other hand, in the more deliberate or author's style, the small letter is more usual. Such personal preferences are not to be satisfactorily accounted for. It may, however, be suggested that the capital *C*, a round letter, is easily written and therefore naturally recommends itself in rapid writing.

Among handwritings of the time it is noticeable that there was often a tendency for writers to prefer one or another capital letter to the minuscule. This habit might be practised to excess and might thus become a means of identifying the hand.

Letter D. The formal capital is seen in l. 13, a sinuous letter commencing with an under-line curve returning in a long-drawn base-line and ending in a large symmetrical loop above the line. But a less formal letter—a large twin-looped *D*, dashed off at great speed—appears as the initial of the character-name 'Doll' which is entered in the margins of the Addition. This modified letter may be regarded rather as an exaggerated minuscule than a true capital—or at least an arbitrary capital. The same form of letter is used by other contemporary writers.

Letter E. This formal letter occurs thrice in the Addition (ll. 24, 30, 31): a symmetrical crescent, bisected by a horizontal cross-bar commencing with an ornamental loop.

Letter F. Double minuscule *f* represented the capital in the old English cursive hand from an early date and was so used in the Elizabethan hand. An instance occurs in l. 127.

Letter I or J. The conventional scrivener's capital used in the Addition is an awkwardly shaped letter (ll. 28, 35, 58, 89), beginning with a small looped head, a stem sloped and traversed by a cross-bar and a pendent curve below the line. There is also a simpler letter (ll. 73, 80, 99, 128, 129) having an oblique stem looped at top and bottom. A third variety, having a cross-bar, occurs in l. 58.

Letter L. There is little difference between the scrivener's normal letter and the modern looped *L*, except that it was generally in a sloping or reclining posture.

Letter P. A scrivener's normal letter stands in l. 1 —a main stem beginning with a small curve and linked with a detached limb representing the bow of the letter, within which is an ornamental dot. Another conventional shape is in l. 35; a compact letter composed of main stem, with bow attached and enclosing a dot, crossed by a curved stroke forming the base of the bow.

Letter S. There are many examples of this letter both in the Signatures and in the Addition (in the margins as well as in the text); and there is a greater variety among them than is the case with any other of the capital letters. The English capital *S* was in fact the most difficult one of the alphabet to write symmetrically. The two alternating curves which constitute the actual body of the *S* are lengthened fancifully by continuing the tail of the lower one and carrying it round the letter in an embracing semi-circle which finally forms a covering arch overhead. The most symmetrical example in the Addition is in the word 'Surrey,' l. 24. There are many exaggerations, written at speed, to be seen in the first page.

[Among the Signatures, the *S* in No. 1 is a perfect example, the several curves being well-proportioned and symmetrical. The faulty character of Nos. 2–6 has already been noticed; here I briefly repeat particulars of the capital *S* in each one (excepting No. 4, where the letter is defaced). In Signature No. 2, written on the seal-label of the deed and therefore in a confined space, the letter is not in a free hand but is hesitatingly formed, the rising curve at the back of the letter seeming to creep upward and then, instead of continuing in a symmetrical arch clear above the letter, as in signature No. 1, it is shut down flat, like the lid of a box, with a heavy hand. Signature No. 3, written simultaneously with No. 2, or not later than the following day, is also inscribed on the seal-label, not in the writer's ordinary cursive hand, as in No. 2, but in formal, set letters; and the capital *S*, badly formed[1], exhibits even greater weakness than the letter in No. 2; and both in the back curve and in the covering arch there is a tremor of the hand.   In the case of both these signatures a particular form of nervousness, as already described (p. 66), may have contributed to their imperfection.   Of the signatures to the three sheets of Shakespeare's will (Nos. 4–6) the last (No. 6), we may assume, was the first to be subscribed. The capital *S* is here badly deformed owing to the failure of the writer's hand to accomplish the embracing curve, first moving from right to left and then from

---

[1] It will be seen (Plate I) that the initial curve of the *S* is wanting, a defect probably due to the badly prepared surface of the parchment label failing to absorb the ink. It seems impossible that Shakespeare could have omitted so essential a feature of the letter; but he may have made it small.

left to right. He succeeded in forming the two curves of the body of the letter, but when he attempted to continue the tail of the lower curve in the embracing semicircle, instead of moving in the proper direction from right to left, the pen jerked upwards in a vertical line, skirting the back of the initial curve of the letter, and only then moving correctly to form the covering arch: which moreover ends in an accidental flick from the faltering pen. The curious result of this failure is that a letter has been produced which may easily be mistaken (as it has been mistaken) for an ordinary Roman capital S. In No. 5 the difficulty of the back curve has been avoided by omitting it, a gap being left between the extended tail of the letter and the covering arch.]

It may be noticed that in many of the examples of the capital *S* both in the Signatures and in the Addition there is a tendency to sharpen the curve projecting to the right, with the result of suggesting a caricature of a human chin drawn in profile. The action of the hand in this particular is common to the writer of the Signatures and the writer of the Addition.

Letter T. This letter occurs twice in the Addition (ll. 30, 55). It is a refinement of the scrivener's formal letter, being a crescent delicately shaped, with a strong cross-stroke placed towards the upper extremity of the crescent, within which is an ornamental dot.

Letter W. A formal capital of an elaborate kind occurs in l. 35 of the Addition, having a sweeping initial curve balanced by a final curve which is attached by a short base-curve and encloses an ornamental dot. Probably the initial letter of the name

Watchins, l. 59, is intended to serve as a capital, although in formation it is rather an elaborate minuscule.

[In his signatures Shakespeare made use of two forms of this capital. The more formal scrivener's letter is that which appears in Nos. 2, 4 and 5 and has the final limb attached to the middle stroke by a base-curve. In Nos. 1, 3 and 6 he uses a simpler letter, in which the base-curve is omitted. In all the Signatures except No. 5 an ornamental dot is placed within the curve of the final limb. In no instance is the letter well formed. In No. 6 the *W* has a preliminary ornamental initial upstroke (see pp. 78, 80).]

Letter Y. This letter occurs once in l. 51 of the Addition: well written with a sweeping initial curve, and formed on the lines of the minuscule letter.

Having now seen that Shakespeare formed the capital letters of his handwriting, so far as examples of such letters have been transmitted to us, generally on the lines of the formal capital letters which were used by the scriveners of his day in the native English script, it is obvious that we must have recourse to the same capital alphabet if we are to attempt to conjecture the character of the letters which remain unrepresented. At the same time we may suggest modified forms, if any appear to be admissible.

Letter G. The scrivener's capital was no doubt used by Shakespeare in its most formal shape; and probably also very commonly the more cursive letter.

Letter H. The formal letter may be conjectured, in which the pendent final bow is attached to the main stem by an arched base-curve; and probably also a simpler form in which the base-curve is omitted:

just as Shakespeare used a capital W, with or without a connecting base-curve.

Letter K. The scrivener's formal letter may be certainly conjectured, which is an enlargement of the minuscule and would need no modification.

Letters M and N. The formal and rather complicated letters of the base-curve type were no doubt used by Shakespeare, as by other writers; but at the same time there is reason to believe that he certainly was in the habit of writing much simpler forms of these two letters. For it is to be remarked that in the Addition the names of the characters in almost all instances begin with a capital, the most notable exception being that of More himself, notwithstanding that he is the most prominent personage in the play. His name is in all places written with an initial minuscule—or, rather, what under ordinary conditions would be read as a minuscular m. But it is now a question whether the letter should be so regarded; for there is evidence that both capital M and N were frequently written, as they very commonly are in our modern handwritings, in the shapes of minuscules, but enlarged. To go no further afield than the other Additions to this play of *Sir Thomas More*, instances of the use of these enlarged minuscules as capital letters are to be found by the side of the scrivener's formal letters. An instance of this use of the enlarged minuscule-form of M, in the hand of the writer of the Addition C, is to be seen in this present Addition (D) in the marginal correction 'Maior' (l. 26). Therefore, when we find the writer of the Addition persistently employing what to all appearance is a minuscule m as the initial letter of the important character-name 'More,' we may hesitate to account the letter at its face-value, but rather assume that it is to be read as a capital. And indeed, every here and there (e.g. in the margins of ll. 55, 61, 144) the letter is written with some prominence, as though the writer intended it to be something more than the apparent minuscule. With the example of the practice of the writers of the other Additions to support us, it seems quite reasonable to credit Shakespeare with the use of the enlarged minuscules *m* and *n* to do duty as capitals, as well as of the scrivener's formal letters.

Letter R. Again the scrivener letter of the more elaborate base-curve type, following the lines of the second form of the letter *B* described above, may be included in Shakespeare's capital alphabet, though probably also with a simpler alternative.

Five letters remain to be conjectured. Three of these may with little hesitation be decided as the letters of the scrivener's alphabet, viz.:

Letters O, Q and U (V). These are not complicated letters and offer little scope, if any, for modification. We may assume that Shakespeare wrote them simply in the scrivener style. The circle of the *O* is formed in two sections and is traversed by an oblique stroke; the circle of *Q* follows a similar construction in two sections, and a simple pendent tongue completes the letter. *U (V)* may be described as an ornamental enlargement of the minuscule *v*.

Letters X and Z. These two letters, seldom called into use, we may conjecture to have been of a simple scrivener pattern.

IV. BIBLIOGRAPHICAL LINKS BE-
TWEEN THE THREE PAGES AND
THE GOOD QUARTOS

By J. DOVER WILSON

WHEN my attention was first seriously directed to the problem of the *More* Addition, I had already, at Mr Pollard's suggestion, under-taken a bibliographical enquiry into the nature of the 'copy' used for the Good Shakespearian Quartos, with a view to discovering if possible something about the character of Shakespeare's manuscripts. At the best, the first edition of one of Shakespeare's plays was printed direct from his autograph; and Mr Pollard has happily shown us reason for believing that this best occurred more frequently than has hitherto been suspected. At the worst, it was printed from a transcript of the original. Yet even if this worst were found to account for most of the quarto productions, such a situation need not lead us to despair. It is exceedingly unlikely that a copyist would obliterate all traces of Shakespeare's penmanship in making his transcript; and the presence of a copyist simply means that two men stand between the printed text and the original instead of one, viz. the compositor. Indeed, the fact that some of the Bad Quartos, which are al-most certainly based in part upon transcripts from an original manuscript, occasionally exhibit passages closely resembling their counterparts in the Good Quartos, in punctuation, spellings or misprints, goes to show that Shakespeare's pen could still influence the printed page, even after the lines of his verse had passed through two heads other than his own.

Lists were, accordingly, made of all the obvious misprints (i.e. misprints which have been corrected in all modern editions), and of the abnormal spellings which occur in the Good Quartos. By 'abnormal spellings' is meant such spellings as a reputable compositor of Shakespeare's day is not likely to have wittingly introduced into the text himself. Many spellings which to us seem archaic were of course quite 'normal' at that period. Yet the spelling of sixteenth and seventeenth century compositors was on the whole far more modern than that of the average author with whose manuscript they had to cope; and withal far more consistent, since at that time spelling differed not only from author to author, but often from page to page, or even from line to line, in the same manuscript. It was, indeed, this chaos of usage which forced the compositors to be more or less systematic; for, to set up a manuscript in type letter by letter would have been not only tedious but costly. Time was money, even in those days; and speed was an important element in the compositor's skill. Further, speed meant carrying a number of words at one time in the head, and the head-carrying process meant altering the spelling. Why, then, is it that abnormal spellings frequently crop up in the quartos? The answer is that they come, most of them, from the manuscript; they are words which have caught the compositor's eye. An unskilful compositor, i.e. one not able to carry many words in his head at a time, will naturally cling close to his 'copy,' and so introduce a number of his author's spellings into print. But even an accomplished craftsman will at times let copy-spellings through—when he is tired, or when a difficult passage confronts him which has to be spelt out. Thus, by making a collection of such abnormal spellings, it is possible to learn a good deal about an author's orthographic habits. In any event, when in dealing with the fifteen Good Quarto texts[1], produced by some nine or ten different printing-houses over a space of twenty-nine years, we find the same types of misprint and the same peculiarities of spelling recurring throughout, it is safe to attribute them to the one constant factor behind them all—the pen of William Shakespeare.

Feeling that I had in this collection of misprints and spellings a body of definite information about Shakespearian 'copy,' I turned, as the reader will understand, in some considerable excitement to the *More* Addition. It seemed to me possible to put Sir Edward Maunde Thompson's thesis to the biblio-graphical test. To take a simple instance: the constant confusion between *e* and *d* in the quartos proves that the copy from which they were printed was in English script, in which these two letters are formed on the same pattern; to have found, then, that the Addition was written in an Italian hand would have been dis-concerting, to say the least. Or again, one of the biblio-graphical features of the quartos is the frequent and whimsical appearance of an initial capital C, in a way which shows that Shakespeare's pen was fond of using this letter in place of the minuscule. It was therefore encouraging to note that every initial *c* on p. 1 of the Addition was a capital, eight out of fifteen were

---

[1] Excluding *Titus Andronicus* and *Richard III,* as suspect, and including the *Sonnets* and the two poems.

capitals on p. 2, and four out of eleven on p. 3. Too much must not be made of this coincidence; the C majuscule in 'English' is a good round letter, easy to form and distinctive, so that its spasmodic appearance is not without parallel, is, indeed, fairly common, in other books of the period. But the writer of the Addition *might* have had a liking for another capital (e.g. for A, which is Gabriel Harvey's favourite letter); and it is reassuring to find he had not. Another interesting similarity between the quartos and the Addition has recently come to light. The three pages of manuscript contain 147 lines: 45 on the first, 50 on the second, and 52 on the third. The other writers of *More* are more sparing of paper; Munday averages 79 lines to a page, Hand A 71 lines, Hand B 66, and Hand C 60[1]. Now, in printing the *Second Part of Henry IV* Sims's compositors inadvertently omitted a scene in some copies, an omission which they subsequently rectified. It seems clear that the scene in question was written upon two sides of a single sheet; and it is remarkable that it contains 108 lines, i.e. 54 lines to a page, a figure which closely approximates to that given us by the Addition. As Mr Pollard, to whom this discovery is due, writes "If anyone on other grounds is already convinced that Shakespeare was the writer of those pages and that he wrote them not long before he wrote 2 *Henry IV*, he will be pleased with the coincidence that Shakespeare in this play and the writer of the three pages in *More* seem to have put their lines on paper in much the same rather unusually expensive way[2]."

[1] The various hands in the *More* MS. were thus classified by Dr W. W. Greg in his Malone Society edition of the text.
[2] *Times Literary Supplement*, Oct. 21, 1920.

Taken singly, of course, coincidences like these prove nothing; they are at best negative evidence. But as they begin to accumulate they tend to become impressive. And when one turns to the misprints and spellings of the Good Quartos the accumulation of coincidence grows very impressive indeed.

MISPRINTS. The commonest misprints in the printed Shakespearian texts fall into five classes. Let us take them in turn, noting the parallels in the Addition as we go along:

(i) *minim* misprints. In 'English' script minim-letters are *m, n, u, i, c, r, w*; and the large number of compositor's errors in words containing such letters prove that Shakespeare must have been more than ordinarily careless in his formation of them, that he did not properly distinguish between the convex and concave forms, and that he often kept no count of his strokes, especially when writing two or more minim-letters in combination. For example, we have 'game' for 'gain' (*Oth.*), 'might' for 'night' and 'sting' for 'stung' (*Lear*), 'sanctity' for 'sanity,' and 'the most' for 'th' inmost' (*Ham.*), 'vncharmd' for 'unharmed' and 'fennell' for 'female' (*Rom.*), 'where' for 'when' (*Oth.* and *Lear*) and 'when' for 'where' (*2 Hen. IV*), 'pardons' for 'pandars' (*Ham.*), 'arm'd' for 'a wind' (*Ham.*), 'now' for 'nor' (*1 Hen. IV*).

The excessive carelessness of the pen which wrote the Addition in its formation of minim-letters has struck every student of these three pages. It is sometimes difficult to distinguish *w* from *r* (cf. *r*yse, *w*hat l. 106; *tw*ere, *er*ror l. 95) or *r* from *n* (v. figure l. 102, tea*r*es l. 108); the letters *m* and *n* are very often concave in form; and the writer's besetting sin is a neglect to count the strokes of such letters, especially when they appear in combination (e.g. Linco l. 5—*in* with two minims; dung l. 12—*un* with five minims, etc., etc.). Now, of course, minim-misprints are by no means peculiar to the Shakespearian quartos, or minim-penslips to the Addition, though we fancy that their frequency in either case is somewhat remarkable. It is, for instance, noteworthy that while Dr Greg called special attention to three minim-penslips by Hand D in his edition of *Sir Thomas More* for the Malone Society, only two others in the whole of the rest of the manuscript seem to have caught his eye. All we wish here to insist upon, however, is that the writer of the quarto-manuscripts and the writer of the Addition are once more shown to be alike in their penmanship.

(ii) *a : minim* misprints. This second class is closely connected with the first, and is to be explained by Shakespeare's habit of sometimes leaving the top of his *a* open, or conversely of curving the initial minim of his *u* so that it appears to be an ill-formed *a*. Thus *Oth.* gives us 'coach' for 'couch' and 'heate' for 'hint' (spelt 'hente'); *Troil.* 'seat' for 'sense'; *Ham.* 'heave a' for 'heaven' and 'raine' for 'ruin'; *L.L.L.* 'vnsallied' for 'unsullied,' etc. Conversely we have 'distruction' for 'distraction' and 'Thous' for 'Thoas' in *Troil.*; 'vttred' for 'altred' in 2 *Hen. IV*; 'sute' for 'sale' in *Rom.*; 'couches' for 'coaches' in *L.L.L.*, etc.

In the Addition *a* and *u* are frequently quite indistinguishable; compare, for example, 'nat*u*re' (l. 126) with 'I*a*rman' (l. 128), and note that the first stroke of the *u* in 'nature' is curved, exactly as if the pen were preparing to write an *a*.

(iii) *e* : *d* misprints. As we have already noted, the formation of these two letters generally differs as to scale only, in the English style, a difference which the quantity of errors due to confusion between them in the quartos proves that Shakespeare was not careful to observe. A few oddities may be here given: 'end' for 'due' (*Son.*), 'lawelesse' for 'landlesse' (*Ham.*), 'beholds' for 'behowles' (*M.N.D.*), 'some' for 'fond' (*Rom.*), 'and' for 'are' (*Lear* and 2 *Hen. IV*). It would be idle to give instances of a similar carelessness from the Addition; they occur in almost every other line.

(iv) *e* : *o* misprints. The small-scale *e* and *o* are very similar in English script; they are therefore liable to confusion in rapid writing. Thus we find 'these' for 'those' and 'now' for 'new' more than once in the quartos, together with 'thou' for 'then' and 'then' for 'thou,' 'euer' for 'over' and 'ouer' for 'ever,' and so on. The distinction is generally well preserved in the Addition. But the second *o* of 'shoold' (l. 81) and the *o* of 'plodding' (l. 76) are formed like an *e*, while in 'be' (middle of l. 130), 'them' (l. 138), 'gentlemen' (l. 144), the head of the *e* shows a tendency to exaggeration, so that in the first instance at any rate we get 'bo.'

(v) *o* : *a* misprints. The quartos give us a few examples of *a* misprinted for *o*, generally where a minim letter follows, e.g. 'frame' for 'from,' 'hand' for 'home,' 'cammon' for 'common.' These may be explained by crowding and are not particularly significant. More frequently, however, we have *o* for *a*, and in words where, as often as not, no minim-letter occurs to account for the confusion. Thus *Troil.* gives us 'obiect' for 'abject' and 'Calcho's' for

'Calchas,' *Lear* 'lodes' for 'ladies' and 'O light' for 'alight,' *Ham.* 'cost' for 'cast,' *Merch.* 'lost' for 'last,' etc. Now this curious type of misprint is very neatly explained by the handwriting of the Addition, where we have frequent instances of the method of forming an *a* in which the upright becomes detached from the body of the letter, so as to give something which closely resembles *o* linked with the letter following, *oi*, or *œ*. Examples of this may be found in ll. 5 (great, eate), 7 (a), 9 (a), 12 (palsey), 52 (a), 57 (masters), 85 (reasons), 94 (thappostle), 108 (wash), 122 (a), 130 (pleasd), 131 (a), 133 (afoord), 142 (master). That a compositor could go the full length of mistaking Shakespeare's *a* for *œ* is proved by the *Hamlet* quarto in which we have 'sort' for 'sate' (1. 5. 56) and 'or' for 'a' (1. 2. 96).

In dealing with misprints i–iv, we are still in the sphere of negative evidence. Such misprints and penslips are common in books and manuscripts of the period, though we think it unlikely that many would be found which would show a general proneness to *all four* to the same extent as is shown in the quartos and the Addition. In any event our accumulation of coincidence goes forward; our confidence is not dashed as it might have been if the Addition had provided parallels to only two or three of the common quarto misprints. But the fifth type of misprint takes us on to different ground. Misprints of *o* for *a*, without the minim complication, are not common, while the *œ* business is probably rare; and though a search through the books and papers of the period would no doubt show that other writers besides Shakespeare occasionally formed *a* like *œ*, it is very encouraging to find that the Addition supports and explains the quartos in regard to this unusual form of misprint. This last coincidence strengthens the case for identification considerably.

At this juncture, perhaps, the sceptic may demur: 'Yes, but how can you tell that a compositor faced with the three pages of the Addition would have stumbled in just the same way as his brethren who set up the quartos; you may have overlooked other penslips which would have given rise to misprints which have no parallels in the quartos.' We cannot, it is true, turn an Elizabethan compositor on to the Addition at this time of day. But we have evidence on the question almost, if not quite, as interesting. These three pages have been twice independently transcribed and printed within recent years: first by Dr Greg and later by Sir Edward Maunde Thompson; and their readings of certain words differ, while in one instance both go astray. I am not now, of course, speaking of words which have become obscure through the deterioration of the manuscript, but of difficulties due solely to the way in which the writer formed his letters. And it will, I think, be admitted that where palæographical experts, with magnifying glasses, differ or go wrong, the Elizabethan compositor working quickly in a poorly lighted room would be most likely to misprint. Let us turn then to the readings in question: l. 9 Greg 'or sorry'; Thompson 'a sorry'—l. 82 Greg 'ordere'; Thompson 'orderd'—l. 140 Greg 'momtanish'; Thompson 'mountanish'—l. 38 Greg 'Shrewsbury'; Thompson 'Shrowsbury,' while in ll. 30 and 32 both editors have 'Shrowsbury' where, as Dr Greg readily admitted when it was pointed out to him[1], they should have

[1] *Times Literary Supplement*, Nov. 6, 1919.

printed 'Shrewsbury.' In other words, the exceptionally careful and well-equipped modern editors of the Addition have fallen into four out of the five traps which most commonly led to the undoing of the compositors of the Shakespearian quartos. This may be a coincidence; but surely it is a very remarkable one.

SPELLINGS. The Addition contains twenty-five minuscule letters (i.e. all but *x* of the alphabet), and fourteen majuscules; on the other hand the writer makes use of some 370 words. When we turn, therefore, to compare the spellings of the Addition with those in the quartos, the field of possible coincidence or divergence is greatly widened, and the argument from agreement, if agreement can be shown, correspondingly strengthened. But before we come to grips with this side of the business a few introductory remarks are necessary.

The spellings of the Addition look uncouth, if not illiterate, to a modern eye unaccustomed to read sixteenth century manuscripts. We are to-day almost morbidly sensitive in the matter of orthography, seeing that correct spelling ranks with standard pronunciation as one of the chief hall-marks of the elements of culture and social standing. The situation in Shakespeare's day was entirely different. Then a gentleman spelt as he list, and only 'base mechanicals' such as compositors spelt more or less consistently. Nor was the spelling even of learned men always preserved from vagaries by such knowledge of the rudiments of etymology as they must have possessed. As proof of this, here are a few spellings culled from the manuscripts of Gabriel Harvey, professor of rhetoric in the University of Cambridge, and one of the most brilliant scholars in Shakespeare's period:

apoticaryes, karreeres, kollege, collidg, credditt, epithite, herittiques, interprit, ishu, meddicine, mallancholy, minnisteri, monasyllables, fisnamy (= physiognomy), *possebly, shewte* (= suit)[1]. If a Greek student and university professor could spell like this, we are not to be surprised at anything we may find in Shakespeare.

In the second place, it should be noted, the probability of an abnormal spelling cropping up in the quartos depends, in large measure, upon the character of the word, seeing that the commoner the word the more likely is it to be altered by the compositor in the head-carrying process. A comparison between the spellings of Gabriel Harvey's manuscripts with those in his printed books supplies ample support to this generalisation. The first volume of Grosart's edition of Harvey's works, reprinted in their original spelling, contains over 200 pages of his writing as set up by contemporary compositors. The following are some of his most pronounced spelling tricks, as evidenced by his manuscripts, together with the number of times they occur in these pages of Grosart: 'ar' for 'are' (o); *-id, -ist, -ith* for *-ed, -est, -eth* (8); 'on' for 'one' (o); *ssh* for *sh* (o); initial *k* for *c* (3); absence of mute *e* after *c* (o); absence of mute *e* after other consonants (41); 'Ingland' and 'Inglish' for 'England' and 'English' (o). It should be noted that 'England' and 'English' are quite frequent words in the volume. The list, of course, might be greatly extended; but these instances should be sufficient to show (i) that compositors freely altered the spelling of their original,

[1] Taken from a list of spellings compiled from Harvey's *Letter-book* (Camden Soc. 1884), and *Marginalia* (ed. G. C. Moore-Smith, 1913).

(ii) that, nevertheless, they sometimes introduced copy-spellings inadvertently, and (iii) that the original spelling of common words was peculiarly liable to be obliterated in print. Yet Harvey's printed works are full of spellings which we also find in his manuscripts, so much so that if his name were not on the title-pages, a very strong case could I think be made out in favour of his authorship. These spellings in print are, however, spasmodic; they are for the most part words that have caught the compositor's eye.

It follows that in Shakespearian texts abnormal spellings of common words are likely to be very scarce or even non-existent. Occasionally, however, a mis-print will give us a glimpse, through the compositor's eye so to speak, of the word in the copy. One or two examples may be taken to show how the business works out. Harvey, we have noted, usually omitted the *e* after *c* in words like 'assistance,' 'temperance,' etc. Out of twenty-eight occurrences of words which we should now end with *-ce* the writer of the Addition omits the final *e* in seven instances. Had Shakespeare the same habit? If so, his compositors, like those of Harvey, covered up his tracks by always inserting the missing *e*; for there are no quarto-spellings without it. Yet the misprint 'pallat' for 'palace,' which occurs in *Rom.* 5. 3. 107, strongly suggests that here Shake-speare spelt the word 'pallac,' forming his *c* like a *t*, as might easily happen in English script; while converse misprints like 'intelligence' for 'intelligent' and 'ingredience' for 'ingredient' can hardly have arisen if the compositors were not liable to be con-fused by such words in their copy. There is evidence, therefore, that Shakespeare, like the writer of the Addition, sometimes omitted final *e* after *c*.

Harvey, again, always spells 'are' as 'ar,' and we may assume that the writer of the Addition generally did so also, since 'ar' occurs eight times and 'are' only once. But 'ar,' like 'pallac,' would be abnormal in print, though common enough in manuscript; and it will be remembered that the compositors in Harvey's selected pages never once give it. How then are we to discover Shakespeare's practice in the matter? Well, the contracted forms 'thar' (=they are) in *Ham.* and 'yar' (= you are) in *Lear* are suggestive up to a point. More significant, however, is the misprint 'or' for 'are' in *Ham.* 1. 3. 74, which shows us at any rate that Shakespeare *could* spell the word without the *e* mute. Similarly 'wer' for 'were,' which occurs three times in the Addition, crops up twice, by inadvertence no doubt, in *Rom.* Like Harvey, once more, the writer of the Addition spells 'one' without the final *e*, and the spelling is found eight times in the quartos. Further, the quartos give us six instances of 'on' misprinted as 'one,' which is a pretty fair indication that the two words were indistinguishable in the compositors' copy. We can feel certain, I think, that Shakespeare frequently if not always spelt 'one' as 'on.'

As a last example of common words which the Addition spells in a fashion normal in manuscript but abnormal in print, we may take 'theise' (= these), a spelling which in passing we may note is very rare with Harvey. Here the quartos afford no help of any kind, and we are not surprised. If we turn to the Folio, however, we find 'theise' in *Hen. V*, 3. 2. 122. Why does it occur here? The answer is that Jamy, a dialect speaker, holds the stage, and that when dealing with dialect compositors with a conscience will follow their copy *literatim*. Yet there is no dialect significance of any kind in 'theise,' a spelling which may be found in almost any manuscript of the period. It is simply a piece of Shakespearian orthography, which the compositor, hypnotised by the surrounding dialect, has transferred to his stick. And the hypnosis did not cease there, for the spelling persists to-day in all modern editions. It is by no means the only instance of a Shakespearian spelling embalmed, so to speak, in the spice of comedy.

The foregoing examples only show that Shakespeare, like the writer of the Addition, spelt certain very common words in a fashion not unusual in contemporary manuscripts, though most unusual in print. We may next consider a group of spellings which had become or were becoming old-fashioned in Shakespeare's day. The Addition gives us 'a leven' for 'eleven,' a spelling which also occurs in *Merch.* 2. 2. 171, *L.L.L.* 3. 1. 172[1], *Rom.* and *Troil.*, while the variant 'a leauen' is to be found in *Ham.* Now these forms, though somewhat archaic, were not uncommon in manuscript; Harvey, for instance, uses them both. They are rare, on the other hand, in print after 1590; and their appearance in *Hamlet* (1605) and *Troilus and Cressida* (1609) is strong evidence that they were copy-spellings. 'Elament' for 'element,' though less striking to the modern eye than the previous example, is probably more old-fashioned; the N.E.D. gives it as a fourteenth century form, but not later. It is, therefore, interesting to notice that 'elaments' in the Addition is paralleled by 'elament' in *Ham.* 4. 7. 181 and 'elamentes' in

[1] This example, which comes from Costard's mouth, is perpetuated in modern editions.

L.L.L. 4. 3. 329. The N.E.D., again, gives 'deul' and 'dewle' as fifteenth century forms of 'devil'; and they cannot have been common in the sixteenth. 'Deule,' however, occurs twice in the Addition, twice in *Rom.* and once in *Ham.*, while the latter text gives it the added support of a misprint—'deale.' Or take another instance from *L.L.L.* (1. 1. 316)—'affliccio,' which at first sight looks like a misprint. The termination -*ccion* was quite common in the fourteenth and fifteenth centuries, as a reference to the N.E.D. will show, but unusual in the sixteenth; certainly not to be tolerated in print. But the appearance of 'affliccio' (i.e. afflicciõ) suggests that it was a Shakespearian form; and we are, therefore, not surprised to find 'infeccion' in the Addition. Similarly 'sealf' or 'sealfe,' which the N.E.D. quotes in brackets as an unusual sixteenth century spelling, was probably Shakespearian likewise, since the misprint 'seale slaughter' for 'self-slaughter' (*Ham.* 1. 2. 132) can hardly have arisen except from a miscorrected copy-spelling 'sealfe,' the *f* being carelessly abstracted from the forme instead of the *a*. Now 'self' never appears in the Addition, but 'sealf' is used five times and 'sealues' once. The archaic form 'noyce' for 'noise,' dated fifteenth century by the N.E.D., is to be found in l. 72 of the Addition. It would be quite abnormal in print, and does not occur in the quartos. But the misprint 'voyce' for 'noise,' which *Oth.* 5. 2. 85 offers us, shows that Shakespeare's old-fashioned spelling was puzzling the compositors in 1622. Further, in *A Lover's Complaint* we find the spelling 'straing' for 'strange.' The N.E.D. gives it (together with 'straynge') as a sixteenth century form, but quotes no examples; it was therefore probably uncommon, and I know of no other instances beyond those here given. Yet we can be almost certain that it was a Shakespearian usage, since the misprint[1] 'straying' for 'strange' in *L.L.L.* 5. 2. 773 can be neatly explained by the presence of 'straing' or 'strayng' (with the *n* perhaps written in three minims) in the copy. The Addition gives us 'straing' once, 'straingers' six times, and 'strange' or 'straunge,' its normal variant, never. Lastly, to cut our list short, we may take the form 'Iarman' which the Addition uses for 'German'—certainly an unusual one in that period. Once more a misprint comes to our help, this time from the Folio, *M.W.W.* giving us 'Iamanie' for 'Germanie' at 4. 5. 89. We may observe, in passing, that 'Jamany,' which is a word from the mouth of the redoubtable Dr Caius, still persists in all modern editions—another instance of the conservative force of the comic spirit.

The spellings quoted from the Addition in the last paragraph are, for the most part, unusual forms for writers of the period. They are old-fashioned; and it is unlikely, to say the least of it, that any two authors would be equally old-fashioned in the spelling of *all* these words. It is, therefore, very encouraging to find parallels in the quartos for every one of them. Our accumulation of coincidences is by this time growing into an impressive pile. Can we crown it by citing a spelling from both the Addition and the quartos which is not only old-fashioned but very old-fashioned,

---

[1] Not perhaps an 'obvious misprint' in the sense used on p. 114, since the Q 'straying,' rejected by Capell and later editors, has recently found a defender in Mr H. C. Hart, editor of the 'Arden' *Love's Labour's Lost*. I am convinced, however, that Mr Hart is mistaken.

not only unusual but rare? We have such a spelling, I think, in 'scilens,' which occurs in l. 50 of the Addition. It is undoubtedly a rare form, and though the N.E.D. gives 'scylens,' which comes near it, among its list of variant spellings, it actually quotes no closer or later parallel than 'scylence' (1513)[1]. Now 'silence' is, of course, frequent enough in the quartos, and as a common noun is always spelt in the modern fashion. In one quarto, however, 2 *Hen. IV*, it is the name of a character, to wit Master Justice Silence; and as such it is spelt 'Scilens' no less than eighteen times! A compositor may do what he will with the spelling of common nouns, but character-names must be treated with respect. The business is eloquent on the question of the relationship between manuscript and print in the Elizabethan era. But it tells us something more. The unexpected appearance of Master 'Scilens' proves that 'scilens' was a Shake-spearian spelling—as it was also the spelling of the writer of the Addition.

The foregoing specimens are deliberately selected for their difficulty. With the other spellings of the quartos and the Addition we have plainer sailing. Nevertheless, lest anyone should suspect that, in selecting our instances, we have suppressed evidence unfavourable to the case for identification, an appendix will be found at the end of this paper which gives a list of all noteworthy spellings in the Addition, including many that are by no means abnormal in late sixteenth century print. These spellings are classified, and their parallels quoted from the quartos.

---

[1] The similar forms 'scite' (site) and 'scituate' (situate) are more often met with, and the latter, for example, occurs in Nashe's printed works.

Often the parallel is direct; at other times we have to content ourselves with parallels from words of the same class. For example, as we have seen, 'infeccion' is not found in the quartos; yet 'affliccio' provides us with an equally serviceable analogy. Or again, we need not be disturbed that the quartos furnish no instance of 'geat' (= get), seeing that, being one of the commonest words in the language, it could hardly escape normalisation by the compositors; yet the frequency of *ea* for *ĕ* in other quarto-words lends strong support to the form of the Addition. Shakespeare's spelling was far from consistent; nevertheless, he was addicted to certain spelling tendencies, which can be reduced to some sort of system; and it is nearly always possible to estimate the possibilities of his orthography for any given word by reference to other words of like formation. Not a single noteworthy spelling in the Addition but has its parallel, one way or another, in the quartos. On the other hand, it is equally important to notice that the normal spellings of the Addition are nowhere seriously challenged by abnormal spellings of the same words in the quartos. For example, the writer of the Addition never uses initial *k* for *c*, or *ssh* for *sh*, or *-id*, *-ith*, *-ist* for *-ed*, *-eth*, *-est*, as Harvey and other authors of the period constantly do. It would, therefore, be disturbing if the quartos gave evidence that such spelling tricks were part of Shakespeare's stock-in-trade as a penman. Happily they do not.

To sum up. We have seen that Shakespeare like the writer of the Addition used the English hand; that he resembled him in his fondness for capital C; that he seems to have written about the same number of lines to the foolscap page; that his pen was prone to all the common slips which we find in the Addition, and to one which was not common; that the spellings in these three pages which are modern or normal to Elizabethan compositors have modern or normal forms in the quartos; that those which are common in manuscript but abnormal in print can all be supported by parallels or misprints in the Shakespearian texts; and finally, that spellings, old-fashioned or rare in manuscript, are equally Shakespearian. Wherever we turn, we discover agreement. We have subjected the thesis that Shakespeare wrote the Addition with his own hand to all the bibliographical tests which seem possible in the circumstances, and every time it responds to the experiment. Bibliography can find nothing un-Shakespearian in the Addition. On the contrary, it reveals a number of coincidences which grow more and more impressive as they crowd one upon another, until in the sum they go very near to proving the identification without reference to other lines of evidence.

APPENDIX

THE SPELLINGS OF THE THREE PAGES, WITH PARALLELS FROM THE QUARTOS

By J. Dover Wilson

NOTE. Under each heading or sub-heading in this classified list the significant spellings of the Addition are given first in italics, followed, in square brackets, by such insignificant spellings of words belonging to the same class as are found therein; next come direct parallels or relevant misprints, where such are to be found, in the quartos, with references; and lastly, a list of indirect parallels from the quartos. Numerals without round brackets denote the number of the line in the transcript of the Addition; numerals within round brackets give the number of times a word occurs. The grouping follows, of course, standard modern English spelling. The line-numeration for quarto references is that of the Griggs-Praetorius facsimiles; for folio references that of the *Globe Shakespeare*.

i. *Doubled final consonant* (generally after a short vowel).

Very frequent in the Qq. with mute *e*, and in that form was a common variant of the modern spelling in books of this period. The double consonant without *e* was apparently also common in manuscript, though rare in print after 1590.

d. *Chidd* 73 [bid 100, breed 10, did 94, dread 99, god (8), good (5), had (4), ꝑceed 114, red 1, stood 21].— no direct parallel.—madd, redd, sadd.

f. *Beeff* 3, *loff* 7, *ruff* 79 [if 91, yf (6), of (13)].— ruffe *Lea.* 3. 4. 2.—cliff (= clef).

g. *dogge* 135.—dogge *Ham.* 2. 2. 182, etc.—begg, cogg, gigg, nutmegg, wagg, baggs, leggs, raggs.

n. *sinn* 93 [an 83, 133, bin 66, can (3), in (7), man 83, men (3), on (5), ꝑdon 143, then 6, 104, when 63, 118]. —sinnd *Ado* 5. 1. 283.—fann, winn.

p. *thipp* 18, *slipp* 122, *vppon* (3) [keep 28, keepes 42]. —vppon (very freq.).—copps, dropps, stopps, proppe, lippes, etc.

r. *warrs* 112, *warre* 113.—warre *L.L.L.* 1. 1. 9, *Ham.* 1. 1. 111.—barrs, starrs, farr, marr, barre, farre, preferre, scarre, spurre, starre, sturre.

s. *prentisses* 22, 23 (2).—cursse, decesse (= decease), pursse.

t. *cutt* 120, *gott* 68, 80, *letts* (3), *sett* 90, *sytt* 77, *whett* 134 [at (5), but (10), Credyt 51, geat 69, great 5, 124, yt (5), Let 90, lete, 43, 89, not (14), out 132, put 119, ryot 113, rout 116, Submyt 144].—gotte *Lea.* 5. 3. 173.— dirtt, fitt, hott, rott, shutt, sott, witts, abette, flatte, putte, etc.

ii. *Absence of final e mute.*

after *c.* *insolenc* 81, *obedienc* (3), *obedyenc* 39, *offyc* 98, *ffraunc* 127 [audience 47, Iustyce 99, peace (15), pence 2, ꝑvince 128, violence 132, voyce 51].—Misprints 'in-gredience' for 'ingredient' (*Oth.* 2. 3. 311), 'intelligence' for 'intelligent' (*Lea.* 3. 7. 12), 'pallat' for 'palace' (*R.J.* 5. 3. 107), 'instance' for 'instant' (*L.L.L.* 5. 2. 817) can best be explained by Shakespeare's habit of omitting *e* after *c.*

after *g.* *Charg* 28, *straing* 8 [charge 55, lugage 75]. —Charg *L.L.L.* 5. 1. 86; straing *Lover's Comp.* 303; 'Strange' misprinted 'straying' *L.L.L.* 5. 2. 773.—chal-leng, mannadg, reneag, reueng, targ.

after *m. com* 124, *Coms* 14 [Come 4, name 26, 103, 115, same 85, 108, armes 95, tymes 66].—com *Ad.* 2. 3. 32, *Ham.* 5. 2. 111, *L.L.L.* 1. 1. 59; coms *Ham.* 5. 1. 153, *V.A.* 444, *L.L.L.* 5. 2. 548.—becom, nam, som, welcom, hansom, theams, Achadems, somthing, sombody, somtime.

after *n. ymagin* 74, *doon* 141, *on* (= one) 62, 83, 87 [throne 103, nyne 2, mutynes 115, stone 3].—on (= one) 8 times in Qq., don *Lea.* 5. 3. 35.—engin, medicin, begon, gon, non.

after *r. ar* (8), *forwarne* 94, *ther* 118, *thers* 147, *wer* (3), *wherin* 65 [are 107, desyres 77, figure 102, nature 126, sore 10, there 63, twere 95, where 129].—tha'r *Ham.* 4. 7. 11, y'ar *Lea.* 4. 6. 9; 4. 7. 49, or (misp. for 'ar') *Ham.* 1. 3. 74, thers (11), wer *R.J.* 2. 2. 11, 2. 5. 16, wer't *Lea.* 4. 2. 63, *Oth.* 2. 3. 349, wherin *Lea.* 3. 1. 12, *Luc.* 1526.— Nauar, plesur, tresur, ventur, vultur, sowr, therfore, far (= fare), etc.

after *s. howskeeper* 58 [case 139, choose 70, ryse 106, theise 12, 67, 144].—houskeeping *L.L.L.* 2. 1. 104, houshold *Ric. II*, 2. 2. 60, 2. 3. 28, *R.J.* (pro.) *Luc.* 198, etc.— codpis, copps, deus (= deuce), els, opposles.

after *t. appropriat* 137, *desperat* 107 [maiestrate 146, state 67].—'appropriate' not in canon, 'desperat' or 'desprat' (10).—adulterat, agat, aggrauat, confiderat, currat (= curate), importunat, mandat, pallat, prenominat, priuat, remediat, peregrinat, smot.

iii. *Doubled medial consonant.*
Very frequent in Qq.

hiddious 132, *apostle* 94.—hiddious *Ham.* 2. 2. 498, 'apostle' (only twice in Shakespeare).

iv. *Single medial consonant.*
Frequent in Qq.

adicion 118 cf. adicted *Ham.* 2. 1. 19.
afoord 133 cf. diferences, proferd, etc.
lugage 75 cf. bragart, nigard, wagling, wagoner.

Comand 47, *Comaund* 52, 99 cf. comerse, imediate, iminent, etc.

hearing(=herring) 1, *Sury* 48 cf. cary, hering, squiril, etc.

v. *Final -s for -ss.*

Writers and printers of the period had the choice between -s and -sse, and it seems certain that Shakespeare generally preferred the former. [-s had come in early in the 16th century and was going out at the end of it.]

mas 58, *trespas* 124, *stilnes* 52 [passe 4, possesse 120]. —mas 2 *Hen. IV*, 2. 4. 4, 21, 5. 3. 14, trespas *Son*. 35. 6, *R.J.* 1. 5. 111, *Lea*. 2. 4. 44, stilnes *M.V.* 1. 1. 90, 5. 1. 56. —chearles, choples, giltles, les, noyseles, opposles, vnles; carkas, compas, distres, Dutches, glas, kis, larges, pas, protectres; darknes, gentlenes, grosnes, happines, lowlines, neerenes, sadnes; cf. misp. 'Loue lines' for 'lovelines' *Oth*. 2. 1. 232; 'chapels' for 'chaples' *R.J.* 4. 1. 83.

vi. *ck for k after n.*

banck 39, *thanck* 59, *thinck* 138 [cf. mark (3), shark 86].—bancke *Ham*. 3. 2 (Dumb-show), bancks *Luc*. 1442, banckes *Son*. 56. 11; thincke *Ad*. 1. 1. 103 —banckrout, blancke, blancks, blancket, dancke, franck, franckly, inck, inckie, ynckle, lincke, linckt, mountibanck, pinck, pranck, ranck, ranckle, sincke, sincketh, stincketh, stincking, winck, wrinckle (cf. barck, barckt, inbarckt).

vii. *c and t interchangeable, before ion, -ient, -ial,* etc. [c was the early form, which t was superseding even in words in which it did not ultimately prevail.]

adicion 118, *infeccion* 14, *transportacion* 76 [ynnovation 93, mediation 145, nation 131, pclamation 117, supposytion 91].—addicions *Lea*. 1. 1. 138, *Lov. Comp*. 118; for 'infeccion' cf. 'affliccio' *L.L.L.* 1. 1. 316, 'transportation' not in the canon.—condicions, deuocion, impacience, impacient, oblacion, parciall, pacience, pacient, peticioner, sacietie, Venecian.—antient, arithmetition, assotiate, audatious, auspitious, gratious, gratiously, musitian, pernitious, physitian, polititian, suspition, vngratious, vitious.

viii. *ct for t.*

aucthoryty 78, 94.—aucthoritie *L.L.L.* 1. 1. 87 (cf. 'sainct' *R.J.* 1. 1. 220, *Luc.* 85).

ix. *c, s and z interchangeable.*

Frequent in Qq.

prentizes 9, *prentisses* 22, 23 (2), *noyce* 72.—apprentishood *R. II*, 1. 3. 271; 'voyce' misp. for 'noise' *Oth.* 5. 2. 85.—compremyzd, dazie, cowardize, eaz'd, incyzion, rowze, etc.; bace, cace, elce, fleach, mouce, Nector (=Nestor), nurcery, ceaze (=seize), cized (=sized), etc.; side (='cide), codpis, cressant, deus (=deuce), faste (=faced), ise, cease (=seize), etc.

x. *sc for s.*

scilens 50.—Scilens (18 times in 2 *Hen. IV*, 3. 2. and 5. 3. for Justice Silence).

xi. *a and ai interchangeable.*

(*a*) *plaigue* 53, *straing* 8, *straingers* (6).—straing *Lov. Comp.* 303, and cf. 'straying' misp. for 'strange' *L.L.L.* 5. 2. 773.—bained, humaine, inhumaine, mayne, plaister, Romaine, taile, traiders, vaine, wainyng.

(*b*) *spane* 128 [against 109, 134, gainst (3), captaine 114].—atwane, bale, catiffe, captane, clame, dasie, gate, male, plantan, proclames, retale, vnreclamed, wast.

xii. *a for e.*

a leven 2, *elamentε* 136.—a leuen *M.V.* 2. 2. 171, *R.J.* 1. 3. 34, *L.L.L.* 3. 1. 172, *T.C.* 3. 3. 296; a leauen *Ham.* 1. 2. 252, element *Ham.* 4. 7. 181, elamentes *L.L.L.* 4. 3. 329; cf. ralish, randeuous.

xiii. *ar and er interchangeable* (medial and initial).

argo (?comic) 5, *basterde* 12, *Iarman* 128.—argo 2 *Hen. VI*, 4. 2. 31 (F.); basterd *Son.* 124. 2; 'Iamanie' misp. for 'Germanie' *M.W.W.* 4. 5. 89 (F.).—costerd, haggerds, hermonious, hazerd, lethergie, noteries, person (=parson), pertake, perticuler, seperation, seperable, steru'd.—clarke, desart (=desert), arrand, marchant, parson (=person), swarue.

xiv. *-ar, -er, -ur, -ure, -our interchangeable*.

Arther 43 (Arthur 59), *offendor* 123, *harber* 127, *mayer* 28, *maier* 24.—offendor 2 *Hen. IV*, 4. 1. 216, 5. 2. 81, *Son.* 42. 5, *Luc.* 612 (offendour *Ad.* 5. 1. 315), harber *Luc.* 768 (harbor *T.C.* 1. 3. 44, *Oth.* 2. 1. 121).—ardure, armour, cindar, conquerour, dominatur, expectors, familier, feauorous, fingard, frier, gossamours, honerd, humerous, inheritour, leachour, lier, liquer, manner (=manor), morter, murmour, oculer, odor, pander, particuler, peculier, pedler, piller, profard, progenitours, refracturie, sauor, scholler, serviture, singuler, souldier, souldiour, souldior, splendor, taber, tenor (=tenour), tenure (=tenour), terrer, terrour, timerous, tuterd, valor, valure, verdour, vigor.

xv. *au for aw* (cf. *ow* for *ou*).

braule 78.—braule *L.L.L.* 3. 1. 7, *Oth.* 2. 3. 328.—crauling, hauke, hauthorne, impaund, paund.

xvi. *-ay for -ey*.

obay 100, 116, 146 [they (7)].—obay *Ham.* 1. 2. 120, 5. 2. 227, *Lea.* 3. 4. 81, 153, 4. 2. 64, *T.C.* 4. 5. 72, 5. 1. 49, 5. 5. 27, *L.L.L.* 4. 3. 217.—cocknay, conuay, pray (=prey), suruay.

xvii. *ai for ei*.

waight 7 [their (9)].—waight *Son.* 50. 6, *Luc.* 1494, *T.C.* 1. 3. 203, 3. 2. 173, 4. 1. 71, 5. 2. 168, *Lea.* 5. 3. 323, waigh *M.N.D.* 3. 2. 130, *Son.* 108. 10, 120. 8, *L.L.L.*

5. 2. 26, 27, *Ham.* 1. 2. 13. N.B. wey (1), weyde (2), way (3), wayed (1), waide (1) also found.—counterfait, daine, fain, forrain, forfait, hainous, haire (=heir), naigh, soueraine.

xviii. *e, ei and ie interchangeable.*

frende 27, *ther* (=their) 137, *freind* 143, *freinde* 90, *theise* 12, 67, 144 [their (9)].—frend *L.L.L.* 5. 2. 844, frending *Ham.* 1. 5. 186, there = their (12), theise *Hen. V,* 3. 2. 122 (F.).—beleue, besedged, counterfet, forfet, inuegled, perst (=pierced), percing, surfet.—feinde, feirce, feilde, greife, leidge, leiutenant, peirce, seiges, theife, weild, casheird, releife.

xix. *ea for ei or ie.*

pceaue 92.—perceaue *M.V.* 5. 1. 77, perceau'd *Lea.* 2. 4. 39.—conceaue, deceaue, enpearced, fearce, pearce, receaue, ceaze (=seize).

xx. *ea for e.*

geat 69, *heare* (= here) 62, *hearing* (=herring) 1, *sealf* 85 (3), 105, 146, *sealues* 46, *togeather* 16 [lent 98, 102, question 21, red 1, sett 90, wer 63, 95, 137].—heare (= here) *Lea.* 2. 4. 137, *M.N.D.* 3. 2. 453, *R.J.* (pro.) 14, *L.L.L.* 5. 2. 302, *Ham.* 5. 2. 243, *Luc.* 1290, 1660, *Lov. Comp.* 54, 197; for 'sealf' cf. 'seale slaughter' misp. for 'selfe-slaughter' *Ham.* 1. 2. 132; togeather *L.L.L.* 1. 1. 211, 4. 3. 192.—alleadge, ceader, cleargie, compleat, creast, deaw, dispearse, Eaues (=Eve's), eauen, extreame, feauor, fleash, ieasture, heard (= herd), ieast, leachers, leaprous, least, leauers, leaueld, meare, meate (=mete), neast, neather, orepearch, peart, preceading, preast (=pressed), reneag, repleat, sceane, seauen, seueare, shead, sheald (=shelled), shepheard, stearne, tearme, teasty, theame, vearses, weast.

xxi. *e for ea.*

bere 40, *beres* 93 [dread 99, earle (3), earth 104, 133,

eate 5, eating 5, entreate 145, great 5, 124, hear 30, heare (8), leade (3), meale 2, peace (15), reasons 85, speake 41, 57, speakes 41, teares 108].—appere, berded, bestly, beuer, bereuing, brest, breth, cheting, clenly, dere, decesse, dred, ech, erle, endeuour, fethers, gere, hed, helth, here (=hear), hersed, ielous, lether, meddowes, ment, nere, pesant, pescod, plesant, plesur, quesie, rept (=reaped), rere, reherse, serches, sheued (=sheaved), spred, sted, swere, swet, tere, thred, tresur, welth, wery, were (=wear), wether, wezell, zelous.

xxii. *-ey and -y interchangeable.*

Countrey 6 [Country 5, 126, Countrie 5], *palsey* 11, *Sury* 48 [Surrey 24, 48].—Countrey 1 *Hen. IV*, 4. 3. 82, *L.L.L.* 1. 2. 123, countrey *L.L.L.* 3. 1. 132, *Luc.* 1838, *Oth.* (7), Surry *R. II*, 4. 1. 74.—hony, iourny, mony, monky, parly, volly.

xxiii. *o for oa.*

coste 76, *grote* 2, *loff* 7, *throts* 120, *throtes* 134.— grote *R. II*, 5. 5. 68; 'loaf' not in Qq.; throte *R. II*, 1. 1. 44.—abord, abrod, approch, bemone, bord, bore, bost, bote, brode, broch, cloths, cole, cote, croke, gotish, grone, Ione, lone, loth, mone, oke, ores, ote, oth, peticote, reproch, rode, rore, rosted, soke, sore (=soar), tode, toste.

xxiv. *oo for o.*

afoord 133, *doon* 141, *moor*[1] (14), *moore*[1] (3), *tooth* (=to the) 76 [abode 133, among 46, another 87, Brother 43, 59, clothd 79, Come 4, com 124, Coms 14, do (7), doing 107, dogge 135, go 125, 127, god (8), gospell 88, gott 68, 80, more 5, other (4), porte 76, remoued 72, removing 70, sore 10, stone 3, sword 103, throne 103, to (23)].— affoord (8), doone (6), too'th *Lea.* 2. 4. 184.—approoue, behooue, coosning, doo, foorde, foorth, mood (=mode), mooue, prooue, remooue, reprooue, smoothred, stoore,

1 For 'More.'

soopstake, toomb, vnboosome, vnwoorthy, woolfe, woon, woonder, woont, woorth.

xxv. *oo for ou.*

coold 64, 67, *moorne* 123, *shoold* (5), *woold* (8) [although 69, brought 67, Countrie 5, Country 5, 126, Countrey 6, doubt 147, enough 10, foule 108, founde 147, hound 122, our (3), out 132, pounde 2, rough 55, sound 89, sounde 117, though 14, wrought 84].—for 'woold' cf. 'twood' *T.C.* 2. 3. 229, 3. 3. 255.—cooch, cooplement, coosin, dooble, poor (=pour), stoop (=stoup), yoong.

xxvi. *ow for ou.*

fower 3, *howskeeper* 58, *howses* 120, *sowles* 106 [for normal spellings see xxv].—fower *M.N.D.* 1. 1. 2, 7, *L.L.L.* 4. 3. 211.—fowle, hower, lowd, lowring, mowldy, mowse, powre, powted, prowd, rowse, rowt, showt, snowte, sower, th'owt (=thou'lt).

xxvii. *-ow for -o, -oo, -oe.*

how (= ho!) 28.—how *Ham.* 4. 3. 16, 5. 2. 315, 322, *M.V.* 5. 1. 109, howe *M.N.D.* 4. 1. 83, *Ham.* 3. 2. 57, hou *L.L.L.* 4. 3. 174.—cuckow, hollow (= hullo!), rowe (=roe).

xxviii. *ew for ue, ieu or u.*

trewe 16, 88, 141.—trew *L.L.L.* 1. 1. 315, 4. 1. 18, *Son.* 125. 13, *Lov. Comp.* 34, *Luc.* 455.—adew, adiew, agew, blew, dew (=due), dewtie, fewell, insewe, glewed, hew (=hue), inbrew, indewed, newtrall, newter, reskew, retinew, renenew, rhewme, rewmatique, trewant, valew, valiew.

xxix. *Miscellaneous.*

deule (=devil) 53, 56.—deule *R.J.* 2. 4. 1, 3. 1. 107, *Ham.* 3. 2. 136 (deale *Ham.* 2. 2. 628 (2) = mispr.).

bin 66.—frequent in Qq.
ymagin 74.—ymaginary *T.C.* 3. 2. 20.
to (=too) 124.—v. frequent in Qq.
Ingland 73, 129.—Cf. Inglish *M.W.W.* 2. 3. 64 (Q. 1).

xxx. *Abbreviations and colloquialisms.*

a (= he) 42 (2), 141.—frequent in Qq.
byth (= by the) 58.—byth *L.L.L.* 5. 2. 61, 474, *Lov. Comp.* 112, *Lea.* 2. 4. 9, 10, *R.J.* 1. 5. 112, bit'h, *Lea.* 2. 4. 9, 5. 3. 19, *Oth.* 1. 3. 407, 2. 3. 384, 5. 2. 355.
  eu̅ (= ever) 21.
  L. (= Lord) 24, 38.—L. (=lord) *R.J.* 5. 1. 3, 1 *Hen. IV*, 1. 1. 49, *L.L.L.* 2. 1. 214, 4. 2. 75.—frequent in Qq. as a title before a name, e.g. 'my L. Bellario' (*M.V.* 4. 1. 120).
  lets 89, *lete* 43, *lette* 30, 42, *letts* 141.—'lets' frequent in Qq.
  matie 93, 101, 122.
  ore (= o'er) 39.—frequent in Qq.
  tane (= taken) 66.—frequent in Qq.
  thart (= thou'rt) 58.—th'art *Ham.* 5. 2. 353, thar't *Lea.* 1. 4. 23.
  tis 10, 93.—frequent in Qq.
  tooth (= to the) 76.—tooth *Lea.* 2. 4. 184, toth *Lea.* 5. 3. 245, *Ham.* 2. 2. 287, *Oth.* 1. 3. 133, 5. 2. 156.
  twere 95.—frequent in Qq.
  weele (= we will) (4).—frequent in Qq.
  whate 9.—frequent in Qq.
  wch 70.
  w^t (4), *w^{th}* 22, 85.
  yo^u (54).
  youle (= you will) 119, 142.—youle *R.J.* 1. 5. 81, 82, 83, *L.L.L.* 2. 1. 114, 4. 3. 157, *Oth.* 1. 1. 112, 113.
  yor (12).

V. THE EXPRESSION OF IDEAS— PARTICULARLY POLITICAL IDEAS —IN THE THREE PAGES, AND IN SHAKESPEARE

By R. W. Chambers

i. *'Degree'*

FREQUENT misuse has brought into disrepute the method of drawing parallels between Shakespeare's acknowledged works and some play or portion of a play which we wish to attribute to him.

But the case of *Sir Thomas More* is peculiar. Here is a history play, the manuscript of which proves that many hands wrought upon it. Now one scene of 147 lines is written in a different hand from any other in the manuscript—the hand called D in Greg's edition. This hand is obviously that of the author, for we see the writer occasionally pausing, cancelling a word or phrase, and then finishing the line according to his second thoughts. However, for an author composing as he writes, he seems to show great fluency. Shakespeare, we know, worked in this way. 'His mind and hand went together: and what he thought he uttered with that easiness that we have scarce received from him a blot in his papers.' These words can only mean that blots were so few that it was possible to use Shakespeare's original draft as the copy which his fellow actors received from him: for the words are written as a proof, not of Shakespeare's care, but of his fluency.

Not all the portions of *Sir Thomas More* were written in this way. Thus, for example, the hand C transcribes, amongst other things, passages which are also extant in the hand S: and, in doing this, C makes the errors of a scribe, not of an author; in beginning a speech of Erasmus he loses his place, writes three words which should occur in the answer to that speech seven lines below, discovers the error, cancels the words, and goes on correctly. Now just as C is here copying from the script extant in the hand S, it is conceivable that he might elsewhere be copying from a lost draft in the hand D. But naturally we cannot prove this. In style, there is a marked contrast between the '147 lines' in the hand D and most of the remaining scenes of the play, good as these often are. Any possible share by D in the play, beyond these 147 lines, is a matter of pure conjecture. Leaving all such conjecture aside, we are concerned only with this one short scene, extant in the hand D.

But of this one scene so eminent a critic as Spedding has said, that if it be not the work of the young Shakespeare, there must have been somebody else then living who could write as well as he. Since Shakespeare's habit of mingling his own work with that of others in his early history plays was so marked as to have exposed him to attack, it can hardly be denied that here is a case for enquiry. The briefness of the passage, together with the fact that the play was never printed till 1844, is sufficient to explain what in some other cases is so serious a difficulty— why there should be no tradition connecting the work with Shakespeare.

So, when the handwriting and the spelling have been examined by experts, and a favourable verdict pronounced, a comparison of the ideas and of their expression in this scene and in Shakespeare's known works ought not to be prejudiced by the fact that similar parallels have been attempted, in cases where there is not the justification which exists here.

The likeness between the '147 lines' and the Jack Cade scenes in 2 *Henry VI* has become a commonplace of criticism. But this is the less conclusive, because the Jack Cade scenes are found in the *Contention betwixt the two famous houses of York and Lancaster*, as printed in 1594, and much of the *Contention* is pretty clearly not Shakespeare's work. It might be argued that 'the writer who foisted certain of the Jack Cade scenes into the second part of *Henry VI*' was also the writer of the 147 lines added to *Sir Thomas More*, without its being held that such writer was necessarily Shakespeare. Can we draw parallels between the '147 lines' and Shakespeare's undisputed work?

Simpson, when first broaching the subject, drew two such parallels, noteworthy, but not convincing without much further support. Spedding and Ward, in supporting the attribution of this scene to Shakespeare, dealt only with the general likeness, without going into details. Recently Schücking[1] has argued that the play as a whole is an imitation of Shakespeare, written about 1604–5. He finds parallels between the treatment of the 'play within the play' in *Sir Thomas More* and in *Hamlet*. But the insertion of a play within the play was not the invention of Shakespeare; it was probably in the *Hamlet* plot which he took over. If More's attitude to the players sometimes

[1] *Engl. Stud.* XLVI. 228–51, 'Das Datum des pseudo-Shakespeareschen Sir Thomas Moore.'

reminds us of Hamlet's, there is nothing more than can well be accounted for by the common atmosphere in which both plays grew up. It is quite different with the parallels which Schücking draws between *Julius Caesar* and the '147 lines.' Here Schücking claims to have proved a real connection, and it is difficult to dispute that claim. Schücking would account for the connection by supposing the More scene to be written in deliberate imitation. But we cannot argue that, because Antony did actually, as a matter of history, succeed in swaying the mob by his speech, whilst the success of More is fictitious, therefore the More fiction is necessarily an imitation of that historic fact. If the writer of the More scene needed any pattern to follow, he could have found it in the speech in which old Clifford equally wins the rebels under Cade to his side. Nevertheless, there seems a fair certainty of some kind of connection between the '147 lines' and *Julius Caesar*, as well as between these lines and the Jack Cade scenes.

But what Schücking has failed to notice is that there are also parallels with *Troilus and Cressida* at least as striking as the parallels with *Julius Caesar*: and, further, many parallels with *Coriolanus*, in the bulk more striking than those with any other play of Shakespeare whatsoever. And many data, such as Tylney's censoring of the play, make it unreasonable to regard it as an imitation of *Coriolanus*. Nor can the parallels with *Coriolanus* be dismissed by supposing that the writer of the '147 lines' was following up hints in Shakespeare's early plays, and so anticipated expressions which Shakespeare himself came to use later. In *Troilus and Cressida* the final result of insubordination is likened to a wolf who must 'last eat up himself.' In both *More* and *Coriolanus* the phrase is, that men 'would feed on one another.' That the *More*-writer, imitating Shakespeare's earlier phrase, should have happened exactly to anticipate his later one, would surely be most unlikely—it would be easier to dismiss all the three phrases as mere accidental coincidence. Yet, as we shall see later, *when we consider these phrases in their context*, such a way out is hardly possible either. And this instance is only one of many.

Before coming, however, to this consideration of phrase and figure, it is worth noting that there is an extraordinary likeness in the general outlook upon state affairs. 'I am of the same politics,' Tennyson once said, 'as Shakespeare, Bacon, and every sane man.' Views shared by every sane man will not carry us very far on our work of identification. But even people, like the late Sir Walter Raleigh, who have little sympathy with the attempt to 'classify Shakespeare's political convictions and reduce them to a type,' feel that Shakespeare is a

passionate friend to order: he views social order as part of a wider harmony: his survey of human society and of the laws that bind man to man is astronomical in its rapidity and breadth: when his imagination seeks a tragic climax the ultimate disaster and horror commonly presents itself to him as chaos: *he extols government with a fervour that suggests a real and ever present fear of the breaking of the flood-gates*[1].

Now when, in 1907, Sir Walter Raleigh described Shakespeare's standpoint in these words, he was thinking more especially of the great speech of Ulysses on 'degree' in *Troilus and Cressida*. There was no

[1] *Shakespeare*, pp. 191–2.

thought of *Sir Thomas More*. But, if we try to
describe the speech of More, can formulas more appropriate than these be framed? And these phrases do
not describe a general temper: language suggesting a
fear of the breaking of the flood-gates is not common
to every sane man.

No doubt in Tudor England fear of anarchy was
peculiarly strong. And playwrights were defenders of
order: for 'Plays,' says Heywood, in his *Apology for
Actors*,

are writ with this aim, and carried with this method, to
teach...subjects true obedience to their king, to show people
the untimely ends of such as have moved tumults, com-
motions and insurrections, to present them with the flourishing estate of such as live in obedience, exhorting them to
obedience, dehorting them from all traitorous and felonious
stratagems.

But the passion, the fear, the insistence upon social
order as part of an even greater whole, how often do
we find these expressed as they are in Shakespeare,
and in this speech of More? Heywood gives us scenes
of popular violence in his *Edward IV*; so does Dekker
in *Sir Thomas Wyatt*; so does the anonymous author
of *Jack Straw*; so do other collaborators in the play
of *Sir Thomas More*. But the method of Heywood,
Dekker and the other writers is as unlike that of the
writer of the '147 lines' and of Shakespeare as these
two last are like each other. To More, rebellion
means not so much the end of the rebel, as the end of
all things:

Had there such fellows lived when you were babes...
                    ...the bloody times
Could not have brought you to the state of men.

More does not stoop to terrorize the rebels, as Heywood might have done with 'the untimely ends of such as have moved tumults': there is no talk of gibbets and the hangman, but rather of the necessity of authority:

> To kneel to be forgiven
> Is safer wars than ever you can make
> Whose discipline is riot: why even your wars
> Cannot proceed but by obedience.

Ulysses, in his great paean in praise of authority, can begin from no lower thesis than that

> The heavens themselves, the planets and this centre,
> Observe degree, priority and place.

What would otherwise be the intolerable insolence of Coriolanus receives dignity from this passion for a divinely ordained authority, be it that of the senate ('the noble senate who, *under the gods*, keep you in awe') or of his mother. It is this which makes his fall the greater when Coriolanus, of all men, stands

> As if a man were author of himself
> And knew no other kin.

It is this which turns his fall into a triumph when, at the price of his life, he raises his mother from her knees to grant her request:

> Your knees to me? to your corrected son?
> Then let the pebbles on the hungry beach
> Fillip the stars.

Let anyone read, two or three times, the speech of More, and the speech of Ulysses on 'degree,' and then turn to the great Tudor classic on rebellion, by Sir John Cheke, *The Hurt of Sedition, how grievous it is to a Commonwealth* (1549). Cheke was a statesman, and among the chief prose writers of his time. In this book of 120 pages he treats the subject at length, with eloquence, vigour and common sense. He never reaches the standpoint to which Shakespeare and the author of the '147 lines' leap instantly. According to Cheke, rebellion leads to a state of things unpleasant, difficult, dangerous, even very dangerous. According to More or to Ulysses it leads to men devouring each other like ravenous beasts or fishes: it leads to sheer destruction. At the back of the mind of both More and Ulysses seems to be a nightmare vision of a world in chaos. This is not common: Cheke comes, I think, nearer to the practical point of view of the ordinary Englishman:

And now, when there is neither plenty of hay, nor sufficient of straw, nor corn enough, and that through the great disorder of your lewd rebellion, can ye think ye do well?

Owing to the rebellion of Ket and his followers

Diverse honest and true-dealing men are not able to pay their accustomable rent at their due time.

Cheke enumerates the evils of sedition:

When sedition once breaketh out, see ye not the laws overthrown, the magistrates despised, spoiling of houses, murthering of men, wasting of countries, increase of disorder, diminishing of the realm's strength, swarming of vagabonds, scarcity of labourers, and all those mischiefs plenteously brought in, which God is wont to scourge severely withal, war, dearth and pestilence?

To Shakespeare, and to the writer of the '147 lines,' the disregard of order does not merely lead up to such commonplace scourges as war, dearth and pestilence. Both More and Ulysses depict disobedience as a more terrible thing: a thing inconsistent with the order which even war demands: a thing leading straight to anarchy. Cheke points out to the rebels that they

cannot expect to enjoy all the advantages and none
of the disadvantages of rebellion: 'the inconvenience
hereof cannot only nip others, but also touch you.'
More makes the same point, but how differently.
Suppose the rioters, by their tumult, succeed in
forcing the government to carry out their wishes.
What will be the result?

> *Not one of you should live an aged man.*

Ulysses leaps to the same conclusion:

> Take but degree away, untune that string...
> *And the rude son should strike his father dead.*

How are we to account for this difference between
Cheke and the author of *More* or *Troilus?* So far as
contemporary conditions go, the realm was nearer
chaos in the days of Cheke than when these plays
were written. The root of the difference lies in the
mind of the individual. And where else in Elizabethan
drama shall we find just that same kind of passion and
underlying fear which we find in Shakespeare and in
the great speech of More?

But the likeness only begins here: if we had no
more than this it would prove nothing. Even more
striking than the similarity of outlook is the similarity
—often even the identity—of image and phrase and
word with which it is enforced.

But before passing on, in the next section, to
examine this, we must stop to ask—Is there anything
unlike in the outlook of Shakespeare and of this speech
of More? For it has been argued that More places
the claims of kingly authority higher than even
Shakespeare would have done.

Shakespeare, it is said,

was far from being a believer in the divinity of kings. He

treats the theory with mordant irony in *Richard II*, placing it on the lips of the hapless king, and proving its insufficiency by the remorseless logic of subsequent events[1].

But what do we mean by the 'divinity of kings'? In the sense in which Richard II appeals to this divinity, neither Shakespeare nor any other thinker has ever believed in it. Richard places his reliance upon miracles:

> This earth shall have a feeling, and these stones
> Prove armed soldiers, ere her native king
> Shall falter under foul rebellion's arms.

We have not to wait for the 'remorseless logic of subsequent events' to prove the insufficiency of this: it is reproved instantly by the Bishop of Carlisle:

> Fear not, my lord: that Power that made you king
> Hath power to keep you king in spite of all.
> The means that heaven yields must be embraced
> And not neglected; else, if heaven would,
> And we will not, heaven's offer we refuse,
> The proffer'd means of succour and redress.
> *Aumerle.* He means, my lord, that we are too remiss;
> Whilst Bolingbroke, through our security,
> Grows strong and great, in substance and in power.

Richard indignantly rejects the advice of the Bishop. But the Bishop's words are consistent with the strictest legitimist belief. Indeed, when Bolingbroke proceeds to 'ascend the regal throne' it is this very Bishop of Carlisle who interposes:

> I speak to subjects, and a subject speaks,
> Stirr'd up by God, thus boldly for his king.
> My lord of Hereford here, whom you call king,

---

[1] Moorman on 'Plays attributed to Shakespeare' in the *Cambridge History*, v. 248-9.

> Is a foul traitor to proud Hereford's king;
> And, if you crown him, let me prophesy....

And then comes an appeal to 'the remorseless logic of subsequent events'—the Wars of the Roses.

The speech of More has in it the ring of peculiarly deep conviction and present fear: the speech of the Bishop of Carlisle has this equally: but it has something more. Shakespeare goes beyond the dramatic needs of the immediate situation, and uses *his own knowledge* of later history, thereby securing to the legitimist argument that prestige which accrues from prophecy fulfilled:

> O, if you raise this house against this house,
> It will the woefullest division prove
> That ever fell upon this cursed earth:
> Prevent it, resist it, let it not be so,
> Lest child, child's children, cry against you 'woe'!

Bolingbroke gets the throne: but in argument, at any rate, the dramatist 'takes care that the Whig dogs should not have the best of it.' It is surely impossible to maintain that the man who wrote this would not have gone as far as the writer of More's great speech goes. What More tells the crowd of rioters—that God has lent the king his throne and sword, and called him a 'god on earth,' is a mere Tudor commonplace. Listen to Cheke:

That that is done by the magistrate is done by the ordinance of God, whom the scripture oftentimes doth call God, because he hath the execution of God's office. How then do ye take in hand to reform? Be ye kings?

By 'the magistrate' Cheke means the king or his deputy. Writing under a protectorate he chooses the vaguer term. But it is immaterial, for he says:

There can be no just execution of laws, reformation of faults, giving out of commandments, but from the king. For in the king only is the right hereof, and authority of him derived by his appointment to his ministers.

That the king, and the magistrates appointed by him, are executing God's office

> Of dread, of justice, power and command

would surely have been admitted universally in Tudor times. The view has, as More claims, sound apostolic authority[1]. It is going much further[2] when Shakespeare makes the Bishop of Carlisle protest, whatever the king's misdeeds, against the claim of parliament to depose him. As to the 'remorseless logic of subsequent events' refuting this protest, we must remember that *Richard II* is one of eight plays dealing with the fortunes of the houses of Lancaster and York. We see the strong efficient Bolingbroke worn into premature age and death as the result of his act:

> God knows, my son,
> By what by-paths, and indirect crook'd ways
> I met this crown; and I myself know well
> How troublesome it sat upon my head...
>   ...Therefore, my Harry,
> Be it thy course, to busy giddy minds
> With foreign quarrels....

The advice is carried out. On the eve of his great victory we see the son's penitence:

[1] Romans xiii. 1–5; 1 Peter ii. 13, 14. For the 'king' as 'god' cf. Psalms xlv. 11 (in the Prayer-Book version, and in Parker's revision of the Bishops' Bible), 'So shall the king have pleasure in thy beauty, for he is thy Lord God' following the Vulgate 'quoniam ipse [rex] est Dominus Deus tuus.'

[2] Compare the view of King James I, as reported by Gardiner, *History of England* (1883), I. 291.

> O, not today, think not upon the fault
> My father made in compassing the crown.

But bloodshed in France avails nothing in the long run to avert bloodshed in England. The saintly grandson is equally conscious of the weakness of his title, and loses all. In *Henry VI*, with its figures of the 'son that hath killed his father' and 'the father that hath killed his son,' Shakespeare had already helped to stage what he now foretells:

> In this seat of Peace, tumultuous wars
> Shall kin with kin, and kind with kind confound;
> Disorder, Horror, Fear and Mutiny
> Shall here inhabit, and this land be call'd
> The field of Golgotha, and Dead Men's Skulls.

Of this field of Golgotha Richard of Gloucester becomes king. And, after all his murders, Richard knows that they are in vain unless he can gain the hand of his niece Elizabeth, the true heiress:

> Without her, follows to this land and me...
> Death, desolation, ruin and decay.

Only when the Lancastrian claimant is betrothed to Elizabeth, is the evil which the Bishop of Carlisle had foretold brought to its end. Richmond's words before his victory echo those of the Bishop:

> If you do free your children from the sword,
> Your children's children quit it in your age.

The Bishop assuredly does not rate the divine right of the king lower than Sir Thomas More. We may say, if we like, that, despite everything, the speech of the Bishop has merely dramatic value, and does not represent Shakespeare's own view. We may believe that both speeches were written merely to placate authority. But to assume that the speech of More represents the real view of its author: that the speech of the Bishop of Carlisle represents the reverse of the real view of *its* author: and that therefore they cannot be the work of one and the same man, is surely absurd.

It is curious that this passage about God having 'given the king his name' and commanded obedience to him, should have caused such searching of heart. It is the one really commonplace thing in More's speech; it is based upon well-known passages of scripture; it is emphasized, as we have seen, in Cheke's pamphlet, in Elizabethan times the *locus classicus* on the subject of sedition; yet Schücking sees in it evidence that the speech of More belongs to Stuart rather than to Elizabethan times[1]. On the contrary, Gardiner has emphasized the fact that the divine right of kings was a theory more popular in the earlier than in the later of the two periods:

The divine right of kings had been a popular theory when it coincided with a suppressed assertion of the divine right of the nation. Henry VIII and Elizabeth had prospered, not because their thrones were established by the decree of Heaven, but because they stood up for the national independence against foreign authority[2].

No doubt a reader of to-day feels that More's speech dwells rather on the claims of authority than

[1] In connection with this theory of an early Stuart date, we may note that both Moorman and Schücking speak as if the life by Cresacre More were a source of the play. This would mean not merely a Stuart date, but a date too late to be consistent with Tylney's censorship and many other indisputable data. But of the three episodes where Dyce had suggested a connection, two are taken by Cresacre More from earlier lives, and the third is told so differently as to preclude the idea of direct connection.

[2] Gardiner, *History of England* (1884), IX. 145.

on its responsibilities. But we have seen how Shake-speare also extols government. It is not so easy to refute the irreverent American democrat when, amid much that is exaggerated and absurd, he writes 'There can easily be too much liberty according to Shake-speare, but the idea of too much authority is foreign to him.'

ii. *Repetition*

But not only does Sir Thomas More share with the Bishop of Carlisle, Ulysses, and Coriolanus their passionate feeling for 'degree,' and their passionate fear of chaos; what is more significant is that in expressing these things they all speak the same tongue. Here again it is useful to start from a fact pointed out by Sir Walter Raleigh, which will be accepted as beyond controversy. Little as Shakespeare repeated himself, there are 'echoes that pass from one play to another': 'I have seen the time,' says Justice Shallow, 'with my long sword I would have made you four tall fellows skip like rats[1]': Lear says:

I have seen the day, with my good biting falchion
I would have made them skip[2].

Certain ideas were linked in Shakespeare's mind, and this coupling recurs with a curious similarity, in spite of differing circumstances: at one time, it may be, in an elaborate simile, at another in a single line or even word. Thus the idea that adversity tests character as a tempest tests ships, is expressed by Coriolanus in twenty words[3], by Nestor (naturally) in nearly as many lines[4]. So, too, Macbeth echoes Richard III.

[1] *Merry Wives,* Act II. Sc. i.   [2] *Lear,* Act V. Sc. iii.
[3] IV. i. 7–8.   [4] *Troilus,* I. iii. 33, etc.

Obviously, in any question of authorship, we must be careful not to be betrayed into the argument that two authors are the same man because they use the same metaphor. Nevertheless, compare the way in which confusion in the faculties of a lover is likened, equally by Bassanio and by Angelo, to a disorderly throng of subjects crowding round a beloved prince:

Bassanio. Madam, you have bereft me of all words,
　　　　　Only my blood speaks to you in my veins;
　　　　　And there is such confusion in my powers,
　　　　　As, after some oration fairly spoke
　　　　　By a beloved prince, there doth appear
　　　　　Among the buzzing, pleased multitude;
　　　　　Where every something, being blent together
　　　　　Turns to a wild of nothing....

Angelo.　Why does my blood thus muster to my heart,
　　　　　Making both it unable for itself,
　　　　　And dispossessing all my other parts
　　　　　Of necessary fitness?...even so
　　　　　The general, subject to a well-wish'd king,
　　　　　Quit their own part, and in obsequious fondness
　　　　　Crowd to his presence, where their untaught love
　　　　　Must needs appear offence.

The one passage was written under Elizabeth, the other under James. The 'beloved prince' becomes a 'well-wished king' who does not relish popular applause: but there is little other difference.

Therefore, if the speech of Sir Thomas More be Shakespeare's, we may reasonably expect More's figures regarding government to reappear (changed to suit the speaker's circumstances) in those passages in Shakespeare's undoubted works where this question of authority and mob-law is discussed. Such passages are the speech of Ulysses in *Troilus,* and several scenes in *Coriolanus.*

(*a*) If authority be impaired, there can be no end, short of men devouring one another, like ravenous fishes or beasts of prey. So Coriolanus thinks:

> What's the matter, you dissentious rogues,
> That, rubbing the poor itch of your opinion
> Make yourselves scabs?...Your affections are
> A sick man's appetite, who desires most that
> Which would increase his evil....What's the matter,
> That in these several places of the city
> You cry against the noble senate, who,
> Under the gods, keep you in awe, which else
> *Would feed on one another?*[1]

If Marcius had been able to make his language a little more conciliatory, he would have spoken exactly like Sir Thomas More:

> Grant...that you sit as kings in your desires,
> Authority quite silenced by your brawl,
> And you in ruff of your opinions clothed,
> What had you got? I'll tell you: you had taught
> How insolence and strong hand should prevail,
> How order should be quelled; and by this pattern
> Not one of you should live an aged man.
> For other ruffians, as their fancies wrought
> With self same hand, self reasons, and self right,
> Would shark on you, and men like ravenous fishes
> *Would feed on one another*[2].

The language of Coriolanus leaps over stages of thought, as we expect that of any angry man to do, let alone an angry man in one of Shakespeare's later plays. But the thought which is explicit in More's speech is implicit in that of Coriolanus, and leads them both to their conclusion in this identical figure involving an identical half-line.

[1] *Coriolanus*, I. i. 168, etc.
[2] *Sir Thomas More*, Addition II, 195–210.

Ulysses speaks at length, as More does, for he too is explaining the result of anarchy, not denouncing it, like Coriolanus. But Ulysses is explaining to a king, not to a mob, so that the thought is expressed in language of more measured dignity. It leads, however, to the same conclusion:

> Take but degree away, untune that string,
> And hark, what discord follows! Each thing meets
> In mere oppugnancy: the bounded waters
> Should lift their bosoms higher than the shores
> And make a sop of all this solid globe:
> Strength should be lord of imbecility,
> And the rude son should strike his father dead:
> Force should be right; or rather, right and wrong
> Between whose endless jar justice resides,
> Should lose their names, and so should justice too.
> Then everything includes itself in power,
> Power into will, will into appetite;
> And appetite, an universal wolf,
> So doubly seconded with will and power,
> Must make perforce an universal prey,
> *And last eat up himself*[1].

The rioters whom More is addressing are loyal to the king. Agamemnon's authority has been flouted, but he is still the Grecian general. Most people would hold that there is no need to trouble yet with any such thoughts as these of ravenous fishes and universal wolves eating up themselves. Shakespeare would not.

(*b*) Ulysses' comparison of the insubordinate to 'bounded waters' lifting 'their bosoms higher than the shores' is an ordinary one enough. It comes again in *Hamlet*:

[1] *Troilus and Cressida*, I. iii. 109, etc.

The ocean, overpeering of his list,
Eats not the flats with more impetuous haste
Than young Laertes, in a riotous head,
O'erbears your officers.

But when we come to *Sir Thomas More* and *Coriolanus* we find this ordinary comparison in contexts which are quite extraordinarily alike. In *More*, Surrey and Shrewsbury enter and try to speak, whilst the leader of the mob, in an effort to still the tumult, exclaims to his followers 'Peace, I say, Peace! Are you men of wisdom, or what are you?' The young noble, Surrey, interjects a scoffing 'What you will have them, but not men of wisdom.' This naturally provokes an outburst from the crowd: 'We'll not hear my lord of Surrey, No, No, No, No, No.' Then More first speaks:

> Whiles they are *o'er the bank of their obedience*
> *Thus will they bear down all things.*

And, at the invitation of the mob, More then tries what can be effected by a less provocative style of address from a man in humbler station.

It is with a similar metaphor that Cominius hurries Coriolanus off the scene:

> Will you hence
> Before the tag return? Whose rage doth rend
> Like interrupted waters, *and o'erbear*
> *What they are used to bear.*

And Menenius is left behind to patch matters on behalf of 'the consul':

> *Sic.*   Consul! What consul?
> *Men.*   The consul Coriolanus.
> *Bru.*   He consul!
> *Citizens.* No, No, No, No, No.

Men. If by the tribunes' leave, and yours, good people
   I may be heard....[1]

(*c*) The third figure used by More is used by
Marcius, but not in the mob-scenes. He describes
Titus Lartius as:

Holding Corioli in the name of Rome,
Even like a fawning greyhound in the leash
To let him slip at will[2].

Now Lartius, who with his troops is in occupation of
Corioli, is certainly holding it like a hound in the
leash. But what is the signification of

To let him slip at will?

We must not think that his love of field-sports is
making Shakespeare carry on a figure after it has
ceased to be relevant. If we turn back 40 lines, we
see Lartius calling together the governors of the town
which he has won by force:

Go, sound thy trumpet in the market place,
Call thither all the officers o' the town
Where they shall know our mind.

Lartius neither destroyed the town nor annexed it to
Rome: it is understood that it 'will be delivered back
on good condition.' Meanwhile the unfortunate
magnates are having a poor time. Lartius is

Condemning some to death, and some to exile;
Ransoming him or pitying, threatening the other;

The picture at the back of Shakespeare's mind is that
of armed force dictating to a punished, terrorized,
puppet government; and this reminds him of a hound
being slipped from the leash, to follow whatever prey
his master chooses, and that only.

[1] III. i. 247, etc.   [2] I. vi. 37, etc.

Now, as has been pointed out above, the rebels in *Sir Thomas More* are not disloyal to the king. But it is More's object to show them that their demand for the banishing of foreigners, urged as it is by violence, is a dictation to the government which cannot be allowed:

> You'll put down strangers,
> Kill them, cut their throats, possess their houses,
> And lead the majesty of law in liom
> *To slip him like a hound*[1].

(*d*) Besides these three figures, used in More's speech to illustrate the action of the crowd, other images are passing through the writer's mind, and though these images have doubtless been used by others besides Shakespeare, the frequency with which these Shakespearian echoes recur is extra-ordinary:

> And that you sit as kings in your desires.

Simpson[2] long ago was reminded of

> Whether beauty, birth, or wealth, or wit,
> Or any of these all, or all, or more,
> Entitled in thy parts do crowned sit[3],

> And you in ruff of your opinions clothed,

'ruff' (i.e. heat, pride) 'of opinions' suggests the idea of clothing, and so is elaborated into a metaphor. So in *Coriolanus*, 'rubbing the poor itch of your opinion,' suggests a further metaphor.

(*e*) Alike in the '147 lines' and in *Richard II*,

---

[1] Addition II, 242.
[2] *Notes and Queries*, Fourth Series, VIII. p. 2, 1871. Simpson also called attention to 'ruff of opinions.'
[3] Sonnet 37.

similar language is used when the king is exalted as the figure of God,

> And, *to add ampler majesty to this,*
> God hath not only *lent the king his figure,*
> His throne, his sword, but given him his own name
> Calls him a god on earth....[1]

> And shall the *figure of God's majesty,*
> His Captain, Steward, Deputy elect,
> Anointed, crowned, planted many years,
> Be judged by subject and inferior breath,
> And he himself not present?[2]

(*f*) Again, in both *Coriolanus* and the '147 lines,' the majesty of the state is compared to the majesty of God or the heavens, and contrasted with the undisciplined impotence of the rioters, who are advised to use their knees in prayer rather than their arms or hands in fight:

> What do you then
> Rising 'gainst him that God himself installs
> But *rise 'gainst God?* What do you to your souls,
> In doing this, O desperate as you are?
> Wash your foul minds with tears, and *those same hands*
> That you like rebels lift against the peace,
> Lift up for peace, and your *unreverent knees*
> Make them your feet, to kneel to be forgiven
> [Is safer wars than *ever you can make*
> Whose discipline is riot....[3]]

> You may as well
> *Strike at the heaven* with your staves as lift them
> Against the Roman state; whose course will on
> The way it takes, cracking ten thousand curbs

---

[1] *Sir Thomas More*, Addition II, 224–7.
[2] *Richard II*, IV. i. 125.
[3] *Sir Thomas More*, Addition II, 227–36.

> Of more strong link asunder than *can ever*
> *Appear in your impediment.* For the dearth,
> The gods, not the patricians, make it, and
> Your *knees* to them, not *arms*, must help[1].

Here the parallels are certainly less striking. In the first case the wickedness, in the second the futility of rebellion is emphasized: in one case prayer for forgiveness is recommended, in the other prayer against dearth. The resemblances *may* be accidental.

(*g*) 'You...whose discipline is riot,' says Sir Thomas More. Jack Cade says the same,

> But then are we in order when we are most out of order[2].

(*h*) Note the extraordinary likeness with which the attempt of the speakers to get a hearing, and the interrupters calling for silence, are depicted in *More* and in *Julius Caesar*,

> *Surrey.* Friends, Masters, Countrymen—
> *Mayor.* Peace, ho! Peace! I charge you keep the peace.
> *Shrew.* My masters, Countrymen—
> *Sher.* The noble earl of Shrewsbury, let's hear him.

Compare,

> *Brutus.* My Countrymen,—
> *Sec. Cit.* Peace, Silence! Brutus speaks.
> *First Cit.* Peace, ho!
> *Brutus.* Good countrymen, let me depart alone....

Or,

> *Antony.* You gentle Romans—
> *All.* Peace, ho! Let us hear him....
> *Antony.* Friends, Romans, Countrymen....[3]

[1] *Coriolanus*, I. i. 69, etc.
[2] IV. ii. 200. This, like the 'argo' mentioned below, comes in the First Folio, but not in the *Contention*.
[3] III. ii.

(*i*) And it may be an accident that the two earliest examples of the verb 'to shark' quoted in the *New English Dictionary* are the one in *More* and the one in *Hamlet*. So may the choice of words by which the rebels are admonished 'give up yourself to form,' whilst Menenius undertakes to produce Coriolanus.

> Where he shall answer by a lawful form.

But the argument of accidental resemblance, to be convincing, must be used with economy. The question is whether the eleven resemblances noted above (five or six of them striking) are not more than can be fairly expected to occur accidentally within less than one hundred lines.

And they do not suggest imitation; many of them point rather to those subtle links of thought by which ideas are associated in one mind.

We must add to these resemblances in the 97 lines, spoken by the exponents of order, the further points of resemblance in the 50 lines devoted to the mob.

iii. *The Common People in Shakespeare*

For the writer of the '147 lines' resembles Shakespeare in the words and conduct of his common people no less than in the oratory of his statesmen. The part played by the halfpenny loaf in 2 *Henry VI* and *More* is obvious; so is the logic-chopping discourse of the rioters with their 'argo': 'our country is a great eating country, argo they eat more in our country than they do in their own.' We have the wrestling metaphor 'have us on the hip,' which, unless Dyce is quite at fault, was used more frequently by Shake-speare than by most people[1].

But what is most striking is that the writer at-tributes to his crowd strongly contrasted qualities, good and bad. Shakespeare does the same: as Tenny-son says, 'It is the glory of Shakespeare, he can give you the incongruity of things.' Shakespeare has there-by puzzled generations of critics, who are unable to appreciate such incongruity.

And, first we must note that in the words of Mr Bradley, Shakespeare's poor and humble 'are, almost without exception, sound and sweet at heart, faithful and pitiful[2].' Bradley is speaking of those two plays where Shakespeare seems least at peace with human nature, *Timon* and *Lear*; plays in which the faithful steward and Gloster's old tenant, the servants and the fool, form a contrast to well-born traitors and time-servers. But, as Bradley says, Shakespeare's feeling on this subject, though apparently specially keen at this time of his life, is much the same throughout. We have Adam in *As You Like It*, the faithful groom and the pitiful gardener in *Richard II*.

---

[1] The expression 'have upon the hip' says Dyce 'though twice [rather thrice] used by Shakespeare, is not of frequent occurrence' (*Sir Thomas More*, p. 25) and again in his *Remarks* (1844, p. 52), 'the commentators are evidently at a loss for an example of this phrase in some other writer.' A good many examples have been collected since the time of Dyce, and one of these points to the phrase having been fairly common: 'If he have us at the advantage, "on the hip" *as we say*' (Andrews, 'A Sermon preached before the King's Majesty at Whitehall,' 1617, cf. Arrowsmith, in *Notes and Queries*, Series 1, VII. 376, 1853). Nevertheless the three examples in Shakespeare (*Merchant*, I. iii. 46; IV. i. 350; *Othello*, II. i. 338) show him to have been unusually fond of the metaphor.

[2] *Shakespearean Tragedy*, 1905, p. 326.

Further, even in his ridicule of humble folk, Shakespeare generally shows a loving touch. The keen sympathy of Sir Arthur Quiller-Couch[1] has taught us to see this even in Stephano, 'in extremity to be counted on for the fine confused last word of our mercantile marine, "Every man shift for all the rest."' And all must agree with Walter Bagehot that Shakespeare was '*sympathizingly* cognizant with the talk of the illogical classes[2].' If Hippolyta is bored by Bottom and his company, and cannot conceal her impatience, Shakespeare did not expect us to see them with her eyes. The story of *Much Ado*, as Shakespeare found it, was one in which all the actors belonged to gentle circles, and the solution came from the confession of one or other of the courtly culprits. Shakespeare added Dogberry, Verges and the Watch. He delighted in them: and in the hands of the absurd Watch of Messina he placed the detection of the plot which had deceived all the nobles, and against which even Beatrice could suggest no better remedy than, 'Kill Claudio.' Further, Shakespeare's love of irony has led him to arrange the order of events, so as to bring Leonato face to face with Dogberry and the detected plot *before* the wedding. If Leonato, instead of dismissing Dogberry as 'tedious' had possessed Shakespeare's 'kindly fellow-feeling for the narrow intelligence necessarily induced by narrow circumstances,' he would have saved himself considerable trouble, at the expense of wrecking the catastrophe of the play.

Despite anything the gentles may say, we love Bottom and we love Dogberry: even Carlyle so far

[1] *The Tempest*, Cambridge, 1921: Introduction, liv.
[2] Bagehot, *Literary Studies*, 1879, I. 146 (Shakespeare).

overcame his dislike of fools as to love Dogberry. Yet when, instead of 'Dogberry' or 'Bottom,' we read 'ıst Citizen,' or '2nd Citizen,' we are very prone to see them, if not with the eyes of Coriolanus, at any rate of a patrician partizan. And it must be granted that in 2 *Henry VI* the picture *is* partizan: the crowd is foolish and murderous. Yet even here, the touches which are most Shakespearian are precisely those which are least venomous. But we have seen that though the crowd in the '147 lines' (with its 'argo' and its economic fallacies concerning the halfpenny loaf) reminds us of Jack Cade and his followers, we are on safer ground if we compare it with the crowds in *Coriolanus* and in *Julius Caesar*, crowds which are *entirely* of Shakespeare's own making.

We may admit that Shakespeare hated and despised the tribunes in *Coriolanus* with a bitterness which he rarely felt towards any of his creatures. And we may admit (with reservations) that in Shakespeare 'when a "citizen" is mentioned, he generally does or says something absurd [1].' But Shakespeare did not dislike absurd people, and demonstrably he did not dislike the mob in *Coriolanus*.

We must remember that the plebeians as a whole (apart from the tribunes) never have a chance of seeing Marcius' bearing to his fellow patricians. All they can see of him is that he is a valiant soldier, and that he hates them fanatically. It is in their hearing that Marcius says:

> Would the nobility lay aside their ruth,
> And let me use my sword, I'ld make a quarry
> With thousands of these quarter'd slaves, as high
> As I could pick my lance.

[1] Bagehot, *Literary Studies*, 1879, I. 160.

Now the citizens are starving, and in arms: it is little wonder that they are determined to kill Marcius, 'for the gods know I speak this in hunger for bread, not in thirst for revenge': 'He's a very dog to the commonalty.' The citizens have no cause to suspect, as we who know him better have, that he is a dog whose bark is worse than his bite. Nevertheless, listen to the second citizen:

Sec. Cit. Consider you what services he has done for his country?

First Cit. Very well: and could be content to give him good report for't, but that he pays himself with being proud.

Sec. Cit. Nay, but speak not maliciously.

First Cit. I say unto you, what he hath done famously, he did to that end: though soft-conscienced men can be content to say it was for his country, he did it to please his mother, and to be partly proud: which he is, even to the altitude of his virtue.

Sec. Cit. What he cannot help in his nature, you account a vice in him.

The second citizen has a charity which should cover a multitude of sins.

The tumult is appeased, Marcius again wins honour in the war, and the citizens are magnanimous enough to support their old enemy against all competitors for the consulship. This comes of course from Plutarch: but Plutarch makes it clear that up to this point there had not been on either side the exasperation which Shakespeare depicts. Such scenes as the plebeians seeking to kill Marcius, or Marcius threatening massacre to thousands of the plebeians, are out of the question, at this stage, in Shakespeare's source. All the greater, you may say, Shakespeare's estimate of the changeableness of the citizens: but assuredly all the greater his estimate of their generosity and forgiveness. Listen to their talk:

First Cit.   Once, if he do require our voices, we ought not to deny him.
Sec. Cit.   We may, sir, if we will.
Third Cit.   We have power in ourselves to do it, but it is a power that we have no power to do: for if he show us his wounds, and tell us his deeds, we are to put our tongues into those wounds and speak for them; so, if he tell us his noble deeds, we must also tell him our noble acceptance of them. Ingratitude is monstrous: and for the multitude to be ingrateful, were to make a monster of the multitude; of which we being members, should bring ourselves to be monstrous members.

The citizens recall a bitter old gibe of Marcius', but only as subject for good natured chaff, half admitting it to be true. And the Third Citizen sums up 'I say, if he would incline to the people, there was never a worthier man.' And though their speech is grotesque, the citizens also are worthy men.

And all this frank generosity Marcius rewards by open scorn, and by a haughty refusal to show his wounds according to custom. The citizens are surprised: nevertheless they do not at first go back upon their decision to support him against his rivals:

Third Cit.   But this is something odd.
Sec. Cit.   An 'twere to give again—but 'tis no matter.

When the different groups of two or three, who have been talking to Marcius, meet together again in a body, they find that they have all been mocked alike, though even here the voice of charity is heard:

First Cit. No, 'tis his kind of speech; he did not mock us.

If we compare carefully the citizens' report of Marcius' demeanour with his actual words, there is no misrepresentation, except on the part of the charitable citizen. Then the tribunes intervene and denounce the 'childish friendliness' that would yield voices 'to him that did not ask but mock,' whilst refusing votes to those who ask in proper form:

> He did solicit you in free contempt
> When he did need your loves; and do you think
> That his contempt shall not be bruising to you
> When he hath power to crush?

Of course, it is because he so badly needs their voices that Marcius has been insolent to the citizens. He is too proud to flatter. It is a proof of the meanness of spirit of the tribunes that, whilst they know Marcius well enough to play on his weaknesses, they never understand his nobility. Still, their argument looks logical enough, and we cannot wonder that, so admonished, the citizens decide to refuse Marcius:

> He's not confirm'd: we may deny him yet.

Which of us, in their place, would have done otherwise?

Now, not only is this not Plutarch's story: it is the direct reverse of Plutarch's story:

Now Martius, following this custom, showed many wounds and cuts upon his body, which he had received in seventeen years' service at the wars, and in many sundry battles, being ever the foremost man that did set out feet to fight. So that there was not a man among the people but was ashamed of himself to refuse so valiant a man; and one of them said to another, We must needs choose him consul, there is no remedy. But when the day of election was come, and that Marcius came to the market place with great pomp, accompanied with all the Senate and the whole nobility of the city about him, who sought to make him consul with the greatest instance and entreaty they could, or ever attempted for any man or matter; then the love and good will of the common people turned straight to an hate and envy toward him, fearing to put this office of sovereign authority into his hands, being a man somewhat partial toward the nobility....

And, to point the moral, North adds a marginal note, 'See the fickle minds of common people.' In Plutarch, then, the change is due solely to the political fears of the plebeians, and there is no hint, at this point, of scornful bearing on the part of Marcius: if his friends err, it is by making too great entreaty on his behalf. Nor is there any question here in Plutarch of interference on the part of the tribunes. Shakespeare has altered the facts, as he received them, to exonerate the people at the expense of their leaders, and, above all, of Marcius.

Then, when he learns that the citizens will no longer support him, Shakespeare's Marcius exclaims, 'Have I had children's voices' (as though he himself were not the cause of the change), and proposes to deprive the people of their liberties 'and throw their power i' the dust.' The tribunes answer by accusing him of treason, and demanding his punishment. Here again Shakespeare has altered his authority. In Plutarch, the people reject Marcius and elect his rivals consuls: and there for the moment matters rest: it is later, as a private senator, and with no claim of

his own to the consulship, that Marcius proposes to
take the office of tribune from the people. Shakespeare's main object in making this change is no
doubt to hasten the action: but it also has the effect
of justifying the citizens. When Marcius, regarded
by the nobility as consul elect, and so regarding himself, meets the opposition of the plebeians by proposing
the destruction of all their liberties, what can the
citizens do, except back their leaders in demanding
his banishment? For 'he hath power to crush.'

Yet, even at this stage, Menenius (who should
know, and who does not flatter the people except
sometimes to their face) believes that, if Marcius will
but utter a few gentle words, it will not only save him
from banishment ('save what is dangerous present')
but even now gain him the consulship ('save the loss
of what is past'). If he will but recant publicly what
he has spoken,   why, their hearts were yours,
    For they have pardons, being ask'd, as free
    As words to little purpose.

But it cannot be: for between the headstrong temper
of Marcius, and the venomous malice of the tribunes,
who deliberately play upon that temper, the citizens
are as helpless as Othello in the toils of Iago.

The fickleness of the citizens in *Julius Caesar*, and
the effect upon them of the legacies in Caesar's will,
have been the theme of many moralists. Certainly
the citizens change their minds. Yet it was a difficult
problem. The world has never been able to make up
its mind upon this act of Brutus. Swift puts Brutus
with Sir Thomas More among the six noblest of men:
Dante with Cassius and Judas as one of the three
basest: yet we blame the handicraft men of Rome

because they cannot decide directly; ay, and briefly; ay, and wisely.

The citizens are instantly carried away by Antony's appeal to their pity for fallen greatness, and by the sincere sorrow of a man for his friend. They are won over to Antony's side before he makes any mention of Caesar's will. It increases their indignation, naturally, when they hear that the man who has been done to death as a public enemy had made the public his heirs. (I am defending their hearts, not their heads.) But, at the sight of Caesar's mantle they forget all, and are rushing off to seek the conspirators, when Antony calls them back:

> Why, friends, you go to do you know not what:
> Wherein hath Caesar thus deserved your loves?
> Alas, you know not; I must tell you then;
> You have forgot the will I told you of.

The Roman citizens in Shakespeare are honest fellows, whose difficulty in keeping to any fixed view is due chiefly to their own generous impulses, and to the faults and crimes of their 'betters.' They are rightly grateful to Caesar for his services to the state. They are rightly grateful to Pompey. When the tribunes reproach them for ingratitude in forgetting Pompey while celebrating Caesar,

> They vanish tongue-tied in their guiltiness.

They cannot help it that one of their idols has killed the other. Quite rightly they do not wish Caesar to become king. Quite rightly, when the conspirators kill Caesar, they demand satisfaction. If Shakespeare intended us to despise the crowd, why did he show us them convinced by the speech of the noble Brutus, rather than by the less noble arguments that Cassius

must have used? Brutus appeals to his personal in-
tegrity. Antony argues that the conspirators were
moved by envy. The people are convinced by each
speaker in turn: and with much reason, for

> All the conspirators, save only he,
> Did that they did in envy of great Caesar;
> He only, in a general honest thought
> And common good to all, made one of them.

If the crowd are overcome, it is by no ignoble hand.
It is right that the citizens should listen with respect
and approval to the rather austere patriotism of
Brutus. But Shakespeare has shown us Antony
standing alone over the body of Caesar, and we see
that though in addressing the crowd he may employ
sophistry, his passionate sorrow for Caesar is sincere
enough. This has its effect on the crowd, as it must
have had on any body of generous men: 'Poor soul,
his eyes are red as fire with weeping': 'There's not a
nobler man in Rome than Antony.' The citizens are
sometimes spoken of as prejudiced. Is it not rather
the case that they have no sufficient convictions, or
even prejudices, to save them from their impulses?
One is reminded of Burke's words on the usefulness
of prejudice. If the crowd in *Coriolanus* had shown
more prejudice, things might have gone better. It is
the foolish good-nature of the citizens which tempts
Coriolanus to his destruction. A more implacable
crowd would have made it obvious to the enemy of
the people that, if he could not control his contempt
of the electors, he must

> Let the high office and the honour go.

When, in the end, the third citizen says, 'That we
did, we did for the best; and though we willingly

consented to his banishment, yet it was against our will,' there is, as so often in Shakespeare, real truth beneath this inconsequent nonsense.

As shown, then, in the Roman plays, the crowd is often absurd in speech; it resents scorn; it is easily swayed and excited, and when excited it is prone to lynch indiscriminately. On the other hand, it is warm-hearted, grateful, and in *Coriolanus* (where alone the question of forgiveness arises) the mob is, as Menenius admits, eminently forgiving. Further, Shakespeare is willing to take liberties with his sources, in order to bring out the noble side. This is noteworthy in the man who put the great speech on 'degree' into the mouth of Ulysses.

And Shakespeare, in a way even more noteworthy, showed this belief in the responsiveness of the crowd to a noble appeal. The crowd that thronged the Globe theatre 'asked for bloodshed, and he gave them *Hamlet*: they asked for foolery, and he gave them *King Lear*.' And, in return, he received 'all men's suffrage.'

Surely, of all people, an Elizabethan playwright-actor-manager must have known what he thought of the crowd. It would have been strange, if the man who was to make such an appeal, and receive such a response, had at any time thought meanly of the crowd. It is not strange that he thought meanly of the baser kind of demagogue. He who had given his noblest, and thereby had become 'the applause, delight, the wonder of our Stage,' had the right to condemn those who seek popularity by an ignoble appeal. But when, over and over again, he altered history, with the effect of making the action of a crowd of Roman mechanicals more generous, I am

bold enough to believe that it is not rash to suppose
that he knew what he was doing.

iv. *The Common People in the '147 lines'*

The crowd in the '147 lines' are, like the Shakespearian crowd, absurd in speech, especially when
most trying to be logical. They resent scorn, and are
stung to passion by the contempt of the Sergeant and
of Surrey. They are easily swayed and excited, and
are in a mood as murderous as that of the citizens
who would kill Marcius, or the citizens who do kill
Cinna the poet. 'We will show no mercy upon the
strangers' they say. More, who has no reason to
exaggerate their ferocity, says:

> you'll put down strangers,
> Kill them, cut their throats, possess their houses.

And, whilst they have all the dangerousness of the
crowd in Shakespeare, they are at the same time made
to speak that peculiar dialect which Shakespeare, with
his ' kindly fellow-feeling for the narrow intelligence
necessarily induced by narrow circumstances' puts
into the mouths of his citizens and clowns. Who can
fail to love a rioter whose grievance against the aliens
is that 'they bring in strange roots, which is merely
to the undoing of poor prentices, for what's a sorry
parsnip to a good heart?' When the mob are calling
on More to speak, Doll Williamson finds a truly
Shakespearian reason why the crowd should listen
to him rather than to his colleagues:

Let's hear him: a keeps a plentiful shrevaltry, and a made
my brother Arthur Watchins Sergeant Safe's yeoman: let's
hear Shrieve More.

This is the kind of argument Mistress Quickly would

have used. But Shakespeare, says Walter Bagehot, 'would never have interrupted Mrs Quickly; he saw that her mind was going to and fro over the subject; he saw that it was coming right, and this was enough for him.' It is so with Doll's mind:

More. Good masters, hear me speak.
Doll. Ay, by the mass, will we, More, th'art a good house-
      keeper, and I thank thy good worship for my brother
      Arthur Watchins.
All. Peace, Peace.
More. Look, what you do offend you cry upon
      That is the peace....

And when More pauses, Doll is the first to show that she feels the truth of his argument.

More places before these absurd and illogical rioters the loftiest arguments on behalf of authority. And he is successful. It is an act of faith, as Shakespeare's plays were, and it meets with the same response.

We have already seen how very Shakespearian much of this argument is. It is an appeal to duty, from many points of view. To each appeal the crowd listens patiently, and in the end gives complete assent. More terrorizes the mob, not by putting before them the penalties involved by the failure of their enterprise, but the penalties involved by its success:

      Alas, poor things, what is it you have got
      Although we grant you get the thing you seek?

The overthrow of authority, he argues, will end in disaster for them. And with amazing clear-sightedness the leaders of the crowd see the force of the argument:

      Nay, this a sound fellow, I tell you, let's mark him.

Then More goes on to appeal to the larger whole. To seek the death of the aliens by the overthrow of authority is to be in arms against God. The effect of this argument upon the rioters is instant. Then, from duty to God, More passes to duty to our neighbour. And here comes the only reference to punishment, introduced, not for its own sake but as an illustration; not as a thing specially interesting either the speaker or his audience, but as a stage in the argument. Supposing the king should be so merciful as merely to banish the rebels, how would they like to be treated abroad as they are treating the aliens in London? And, again, with amazing magnanimity, the rebels agree:

> Faith a says true, let us do as we may be done by.

Then, as they surrender, the rebels entreat More to stand their friend and procure their pardon. More refers them to the Lord Mayor, and the great nobles whom they had just shouted down,

> Submit you to these noble gentlemen,
> Entreat their mediation to the king,
> Give up yourself to form, obey the magistrate,
> And there's no doubt but mercy may be found,
> If you so seek it.

More is merely sheriff: in the presence of superior officers he cannot promise pardon, but refers the crowd hopefully to those in authority.

Now the writer of the '147 lines' is not responsible for having made the rioters listen to reason in the words of More. That, though not historical, was part of the prearranged plot to which he had to write. But he *is* responsible for the loftiness of the arguments which he puts into the mouth of More, and to which he makes the crowd assent. The obvious thing to have dwelt upon would have been the fear of punishment and the hope of pardon.

The first version of More's speech—the version which was superseded by the '147 lines'—is almost all lost. But in More's soliloquy beforehand, what he is thinking of is   the law's debt
                    Which hangs upon their lives,

and the fact that unthinking men who join a rebellion
                                incur
            Self penalty with those that raised this stir[1].

Three lines of a speech in which the rebels are per-suaded to surrender are preserved:

To persist in it, is present death; but if you yield yourselves, no doubt what punishment you in simplicity have incurred, his highness in mercy will most graciously pardon[2].
All. We yield, and desire his highness' mercy.
                    [*They lay by their weapons.*

References in the other scenes make it clear that, in the first draft, what More did was to secure, in ex-change for a promise of pardon, the surrender of the crowd, terrorized by the threat of present death.

Nothing could be more unlike this than the argu-ments which in the '147 lines' appeal to the crowd. The appeal is to generosity, fair-play, pity; to those motives which orators as dissimilar as More, Menenius, and Antony know will sway a crowd which is 'sound and sweet at heart, faithful and pitiful.' And all the time, the same writer is laughing at the absurd want of logic of this same crowd. More must be listened to

----

[1] Addition II, 112, etc.
[2] ll. *473–6.

because 'a made my brother Arthur Watchins Sergeant Safe's yeoman.'

v. *Conclusion*

Now a passionate advocacy of authority, such as we find in the speeches of Ulysses and of More, is likely enough to be combined with such keen feeling of 'the instability and absurdity of the crowd as we find in the same scene in *More*, or in *Coriolanus*, or in *Julius Caesar*. But it *is* remarkable to find it combined with such confidence in the generosity of the common people as we also find in these three plays. Was such a view common at any period of history? It is assuredly not the view that Shakespeare is in the habit of putting dramatically into the mouth of either aristocrat or demagogue. Menenius comes near it. And Menenius is one of those characters of whom one feels that Shakespeare approved; and never more so than when Menenius summed up the character of the citizens in a dozen words exactly corresponding to Shakespeare's picture of them: 'they have pardons, being asked, as free as words to little purpose.' But this breadth of view is uncommon.

Shakespeare's aristocrats as a class are more prone to dwell upon the faults of the rabble than upon their generosity or forgiveness. And accordingly recent critics have represented Shakespeare as an enemy of the people, and contrasted him with other English poets, above all with Milton 'as to whose fidelity to democracy there can indeed be no question.' It is often forgotten that this denunciation of the crowd is a commonplace of English poetry: of Chaucer with his 'stormy peple unsad and ever untrewe': of Spenser with his 'raskal meny': of Milton to whom the people are 'a herd confused, a miscellaneous rabble'

Of whom to be dispraised were no small praise[1].

There is, however, this essential difference. Shakespeare puts his bitter words into the mouth of the blunt Casca, or of Coriolanus or Cleopatra in their wrath. As Dr Bradley points out, his noblest characters do not use language like this. But Chaucer and Spenser are speaking in their own persons. And Milton does not scruple to put his words of cold and biting contempt into the mouth of Christ himself.

What is peculiar about Shakespeare is not that he can see where the crowd goes wrong, but that he can see where it goes right: and above and beyond all, what is characteristic of him and of the author of the '147 lines' is the ability to see both things together. It is not so with his contemporaries. Before they draw a mob-scene, they make up their minds whether they are in sympathy with the mob, or out of sympathy. If they are out of sympathy, we get mob-scenes like those in *Jack Straw*, or Heywood's *Edward IV*, in which the bad qualities of the mob are depicted without relief[2]. If they are in sympathy, then we have such a picture as that given in the other mob-scenes of *Sir Thomas More*, where the playwrights treat with respect not only the general attitude of the rioters, but for the most part the actual words in which they explain themselves. In these

    [1] See the excellent article by Prof. Frederick Tupper on 'The Shaksperean Mob,' *Pub. Mod. Lang. Assoc. Amer.* XXVII. 486–523 (1912).
    [2] I take it that the bearing of the citizens in *Philaster* (Act V. Sc. iv.) is deliberately assumed to impress Pharamond with fear of the 'wild cannibals' into whose hands he has fallen

other scenes the prentices may break into slang and catchwords, and the clown may crack clownish jokes, but the leaders of the mob make plain, straightforward, sensible speeches. The dramatist makes them say what he in their place would have said. When we turn to the '147 lines,' Lincoln and Doll Williamson are different people. It is not that the author of the '147 lines' does not think as highly of Doll and Lincoln as the other writers. He does. The magnanimity of the argument More is about to address to them, and to which they are to respond, is a proof. But in the meantime he makes them talk typical Shakespearian nonsense.

Now this mixture, so far as I know, is quite peculiar to Shakespeare.

In his treatment of that kind of politics which is inwoven with human nature (says Coleridge), Shakespeare is quite peculiar....Hence you will observe the good-nature with which he seems always to make sport with the passions and follies of a mob, as with an irrational animal. He is never angry with it, but hugely content with holding up its absurdities to its face; and sometimes you may trace a tone of almost affectionate superiority, *something like that in which a father speaks of the rogueries of a child.*

That Coleridge is right in judging this attitude to be peculiar, is proved by Shakespeare's critics. For the most part they cannot conceive it possible that a man should, at the same time, laugh at the crowd and love it. The greatest Shakespearian critics have assured us that because in *Coriolanus* and elsewhere, Shakespeare shows dislike for mob-orators, hatred of mob-violence and amusement at mob-logic, therefore he disliked and despised the mob. So Hazlitt on *Coriolanus*:

Shakespear...seems to have spared no occasion of baiting the rabble....The whole dramatic moral of *Coriolanus* is that those who have little shall have less, and that those who have much shall take all that others have left. The people are poor; therefore they ought to be starved....They are ignorant; therefore they ought not to be allowed to feel that they want food, or clothing, or rest—that they are enslaved, oppressed and miserable.

So, from a very different point of view, Walter Bagehot:

The author of *Coriolanus* never believed in a mob, and did something towards preventing anybody else from doing so. ...You will generally find that when a 'citizen' is mentioned, he does or says something absurd. Shakespeare had a clear perception that it is possible to bribe a class as well as an individual, and that personal obscurity is but an insecure guarantee for political disinterestedness.

> Moreover, he hath left you all his walks,
> His private arbours and new planted orchards
> On this side Tiber.

Dowden enters a caveat to the effect that the 'citizens' do not always say absurd things, and he reminds us, justly, of the citizens in *Richard III*. But otherwise he accepts Bagehot's view of the crowd in *Coriolanus* and *Julius Caesar*, and quotes it at length. (Yet Dowden insists also on the good and kindly instincts of the crowd in *Coriolanus*.)

Sir Sidney Lee speaks of the emphasis laid (in *Coriolanus*) on the ignoble temper of the rabble, even though he points out later that the faults of the aristocratic temper are equally censured.

Sir Walter Raleigh classes *Julius Caesar* and *Coriolanus* with 2 *Henry VI*, as plays in which 'the common people are made ludicrous and foolish,' without hinting that in the two Roman plays the common people show other characteristics than absurdity and folly.

' Here (in *Coriolanus*),' says Prof. Schelling, ' even more pronouncedly than in *Caesar* and elsewhere, have we Shakespeare's contemptuous attitude towards the mob, which he regards as a thing utterly thoughtless, fickle, and imbecile.'

' The great mind of Shakespeare,' says Mr Masefield, speaking of *Coriolanus*, ' brooding on the many forms of treachery, found nothing more treacherous than the mob.'

Georg Brandes assures us that ' the good qualities and virtues of the people do not exist for Shakespeare ' and that he ' seized every opportunity to flout the lower classes; he always gave a satirical and repellent picture of them as a mass.'

A short treatise, written in order to prove Shakespeare the consistent enemy of the people, has achieved the unusual honour of being within a year translated into French and German, and further of having inspired Tolstoi to write his indictment of Shakespeare's works as 'trivial, immoral, and positively bad.' And Tolstoi's indictment has encouraged Mr Bernard Shaw to denounce 'Shakespeare's snobbery,' 'his vulgar prejudices,' 'his ignorance,' 'his weakness and incoherence as a thinker.'

Here we may draw the line.

But others, like Stopford Brook, perceiving that Shakespeare makes the crowd behave quite generously, would therefore see in *Coriolanus* 'the artistic record of the victory of a people, unrighteously oppressed, over their oppressor.' So the tragedy of mother and son is turned into a party pamphlet: 'Shakespeare, but not so openly as to offend his patrons, was in sympathy

with the people': we may make Shakespeare a hypo-
crite and a coward, if only thereby we can acquit him
of being a Conservative.

It is the rarest thing to find a critic, like Mr A. C.
Bradley[1], who does not deny Shakespeare's sympathy
with one side or the other. Yet this sympathy is
demonstrable. It becomes doubly sure when we compare *Coriolanus* with Plutarch. The brief comparison
I have outlined above was made without reference to
Mr MacCallum's *Shakespeare's Roman Plays*. But,
if the reader is not convinced by my statement, let
him turn to Mr MacCallum (pp. 484–548). There
he will find the comparison set out more fully and
more ably than I have drawn it. In view of this
comparison, there can be no possible doubt that Mr
Bradley is right, when he says that

the Roman citizens are fundamentally good-natured, like
the Englishmen they are, and have a humorous conscious-
ness of their own weaknesses. They are, beyond doubt,
mutable, and in that sense untrustworthy; but they are not
by nature ungrateful, or slow to admire their bitterest
enemy. False charges and mean imputations come from
their leaders, not from them.

Now, the scene added to *Sir Thomas More*, brief
as it is, displays these good and the bad characteristics
of the crowd in such stark and glaring contrast that
even the most partizan of us cannot deny the presence
of both. Let us, for the moment, lay aside all question
of the authorship of the *More*-lines. Whoever wrote
them, they suffice to show that an Elizabethan
dramatist might possess all Shakespeare's sense for
'degree': that further he might make a mob act as
violently, talk as absurdly, and change as rapidly as

[1] A moderate view is also taken by Mr H. N. Hudson.

the mob talk, act and change in Shakespeare; and that nevertheless he might remain convinced of the goodness of heart of the mob, and the certainty of its appreciating the case for generosity and moderation, if such case is honestly put. For that is the whole drift of the scene. We see an honest man telling the crowd what he holds to be the truth, however unpalatable that truth may be: and the crowd proceed to act on it.

Having grasped this fact, let us turn again to Shakespeare. If such impartiality was possible for the author of the *More*-scene, why is it impossible for Shakespeare? And a careful reading shows that Shakespeare *is* equally impartial: takes in fact exactly the same view. A study of the *More*-scene should enable us, babes and sucklings, to avoid an error into which the most wise and prudent of critics have fallen.

Now, if a new passage of Shakespeare's writing were discovered, what might reasonably be expected of it is this: that (whether we recognised it as the work of Shakespeare or not) it would throw light upon, and add to our appreciation of, those passages in the known works of Shakespeare which are most nearly parallel. And this is just what the *More*-scene does.

VI

ILL MAY DAY

BEING SCENES FROM THE PLAY OF

SIR THOMAS MORE

VII

SPECIAL TRANSCRIPT

OF THE

THREE PAGES

EDITED BY W. W. GREG

VI

Note on the Text

THE following is an attempt to supply a consecutive and more or less readable text of the insurrection scenes of *More* after they had undergone extensive revision and were in the form in which, so it is contended, they were submitted to the Censor. His comments thereon will be found in the footnotes. The original is written in four several hands which differ widely from one another not only in appearance but in their habits of spelling, punctuation and all graphic details. Only complete normalization could have produced a uniform text, and in this the whole character of the original would have been lost. Some lack of uniformity in the following pages was judged a lesser evil: at the same time an attempt has been made to avoid mere eccentricity. The very erratic distinction in the use of English and Italian script, in which two out of the four hands indulge, has been ignored; contractions, particularly common in D, have been expanded. In the use of capital letters and to a lesser extent of punctuation some latitude has been allowed: for instance speeches have been made to begin with a capital and end with a stop and proper names have been capitalized: at the same time it has been sought to preserve the general usage of each hand in these respects. Mutilations in the manuscript have been indicated by rows of dots of a length corresponding to the original lacuna, or else the missing words have been conjecturally supplied within brackets. Brackets also distinguish a few accidental omissions of the scribes, and likewise supplementary headings. The original spelling has, of course, been faithfully preserved, and anyone who cares to compare the habits that distinguish Munday, and hands B and D respectively, will find I think an interesting field of study. It is perhaps worth remembering that Munday, whose spelling is almost regular and (but for his trick of writing 'looue' etc.) astonishingly modern, had been apprenticed to a printer.

[ILL MAY DAY

SCENES FROM] THE BOOKE OF

SIR THOMAS MOORE

[SCENE I.—A street in the City.]

Enter at one end Iohn Lincolne with [the two Bettses] FOL. 3*a*
*together, at the other end enters Fraunces de [Barde, and
Doll] a lustie woman, he haling her by the arme.*

Doll. Whether wilt thou hale me?

Bard. Whether I please, thou art my prize and I pleade
purchase of thee.

Doll. Purchase of me? away ye rascall, I am an honest
plaine carpenters wife and thoughe I haue no
beautie to like a husband yet whatsoeuer is mine
scornes to stoupe to a straunger: hand off then
when I bid thee.

Bard. Goe with me quietly, or Ile compell thee.

Doll. Compell me ye dogges face? thou thinkst thou 10
hast the goldsmithes wife in hand, whom thou
enticedst from her husband with all his plate, and
when thou turndst her home to him againe,
madste him (like an asse) pay for his wifes boorde.

Bard. So will I make thy husband too, if please me.

Fol. 3*a*. In the margin the censor has written the note:
'Leaue out ye insurrection wholy & ye Cause ther off & begin
w^t Sr Tho: Moore att ye mayors sessions w^t a reportt afterwards
off his good servic don being Shriue off Londō vppō a mutiny
Agaynst ye Lūbards only by A shortt reportt & nott otherwise
att your own perrilles E Tyllney'.

Sc. i. Part of the original text in the handwriting of Anthony
Munday.

Enter Caueler with a paire of dooues, Williamson
the carpenter and Sherwin following him.

Doll. Here he comes himselfe, tell him so if thou darste.

Caue. Followe me no further, I say thou shalt not haue
them.

Wil. I bought them in Cheapeside, and paide my
monie for them.   20

Sher. He did Sir indeed, and you offer him wrong,
bothe to take them from him, and not restore
him his monie neither.

Caue. If he paid for them, let it suffise that I possesse
them, beefe and brewes may serue such hindes,
are piggions meate for a coorse carpenter?

Lin. It is hard when Englishmens pacience must be
thus ietted on by straungers and they not dare to
reuendge their owne wrongs.

Geo. Lincolne, lets beate them downe, and beare no   30
more of these abuses.

Lin. We may not Betts, be pacient and heare more.

Doll. How now husband? what, one straunger take
thy food from thee, and another thy wife? bir
Lady flesh and blood I thinke can hardly brooke
that.

Lin. Will this geere neuer be otherwise? must these
wrongs be thus endured?

Geo. Let vs step in, and help to reuendge their iniurie.

Bard. What art thou that talkest of reuendge? my Lord   40
Ambassadour shall once more make your Maior
haue a check, if he punishe thee not for this
saucie presumption.

27. From this line on practically the whole of the scene has
been marked for omission (by having a line drawn down the
margin) and 27–9, 33–9 have been crossed out as well, apparently
by Tilney.

Wil. Indeed my Lord Maior, on the Ambassadours complainte, sent me to Newgate one day, because (against my will) I tooke the wall of a straunger. You may doo anything, the goldsmiths wife, and mine now must be at your commaundment.

Geo. The more pacient fooles are ye bothe to suffer it. 50

Bard. Suffer it? mend it thou or he if ye can or dare, I tell thee fellowe, and she were the Maior of Londons wife, had I her once in my possession, I would keep her in spite of him that durst say nay.

Geo. I tell thee Lombard, these wordes should cost thy best cappe, were I not curbd by dutie and obedience. The Maior of Londons wife? Oh God, shall it be thus?

Doll. Why Bettes, am not I as deare to my husband, as my Lord Maiors wife to him, and wilt thou 60 so neglectly suffer thine owne shame? Hands off proude stranger or [by] him that bought me, if mens milkie harts dare not strike a straunger, yet women will beate them downe, ere they beare these abuses.

Bard. Mistresse, I say you shall along with me.

Doll. Touche not Doll Williamson, least she lay thee along on Gods deare earthe. *(to Caueler.)* And you Sir, that allow such coorse cates to carpenters, whilste pidgions which they pay for, must serue 70 your daintie appetite: deliuer them back to my husband again or Ile call so many women to myne assistance, as weele not leaue one inche vntorne of thee. If our husbands must be brideled by lawe, and forced to beare your wrongs, their wiues will be a little lawelesse, and soundly beate ye.

Caue. Come away de Bard, and let vs goe complaine
to my Lord Ambassadour.   *Exeunt ambo.*

Doll. I, goe, and send him among vs, and weele giue 80
him his welcome too. I am ashamed that free-
borne Englishmen, hauing beatten straungers
within their owne boun[ds] should thus be
brau'de and abusde by them at home.

Sher. It is not our lack of courage in the cause, but the
strict obedience that we are bound too: I am the
goldsmith whose wrongs you talkte of, but how
to redresse yours or mine owne, is a matter beyond all our abilities.

Lin. Not so, not so my good freends, I, though a 90
meane man, a broaker by profession and namd
Iohn Lincolne, haue long time winckt at these
vilde ennormitees with mighty impacience, and,
as these two bretheren heere (Betses by name)
can witnesse with losse of mine owne liffe would
gladly remedie them.

Geo. And he is in a good forwardnesse I tell ye, if all
hit right.

Doll. As how, I pre thee? tell it to Doll Williamson.

Lin. You knowe the Spittle Sermons begin the next 100
weeke, I haue drawne a [bill] of our wrongs,
and the straungers insolencies.

Geo. Which he meanes the preachers shall there
openly publishe in the pulpit.

Wil. Oh but that they would, yfaith it would tickle
our straungers thorowly.

Doll. I, and if you men durst not vndertake it before
God we women [would. Take] an honest
woman from her husband why it is intollerable.

92. *winckt*] *t* added, perhaps by C.

Sher. But how finde ye the preachers affected to [our 110
     proceeding?]
Lin. Maister Doctor Standish............................
     ....
     ....
     [re]forme it and doubts not but happie successe Fol. 3*b*
     will ensu...............our wrongs. You shall
     perceiue ther's no hurt in the bill, heer's a copie
     of it, I pray ye, heare it.
All. With all our harts, for Gods sake read it.
Lin. (*reads*) To you all the worshipfull lords and 120
     maisters of this Cittie, that will take compassion
     ouer the poore people your neighbours, and also
     of the greate importable hurts, losses and hinder-
     aunces, wherof proceedeth extreame pouertie to
     all the Kings subiects, that inhabite within this
     Cittie and subburbs of the same. For so it is that
     aliens and straungers eate the bread from the
     fatherlesse children, and take the liuing from all
     the artificers, and the entercourse from all mer-
     chants wherby pouertie is so much encreased, 130
     that euery man bewayleth the miserie of other,
     for craftsmen be brought to beggerie, and mer-
     chants to needines. Wherfore, the premisses con-
     sidered, the redresse must be of the commons,
     knit and vnited to one parte. And as the hurt
     and damage greeueth all men, so must all men see
     to their willing power for remedie, and not suffer
     the sayde aliens in their wealth, and the naturall
     borne men of this region to come to confusion.
Doll. Before God, tis excellent, and Ile maintaine the 140
     suite to be honest.
Sher. Well, say tis read, what is your further meaning
     in the matter?

Geo. What? marie list to me. No doubt but this will
store vs with freends enow, whose names we will
closely keepe in writing, and on May day next in
the morning weele goe foorth a Maying, but
make it the wurst May day for the straungers
that euer they sawe: how say ye? doo ye subscribe, or are ye faintharted reuolters.   150

Doll. Holde thee George Bettes, ther's my hand and
my hart, by the Lord Ile make a captaine among
ye, and doo somewhat to be talke of for euer
after.

Wil. My maisters, ere we parte, lets freendly goe and
drinke together, and sweare true secrecie vppon
our liues.

Geo. There spake an angell, come, let vs along then.
                                        Exeunt.

[SCENE II, the Mayor's Sessions, has no connexion
with Ill May Day.]

[SCENE III. The Council Chamber.]

Enter the Earles of Shrewesburie and Surrie, Sir FOL. 5a
Thomas Palmer and Sir Roger Cholmeley.

Shrew. My Lord of Surrey, and Sir Thomas Palmer,
might I with pacience tempte your graue ad-
uise?
I tell ye true, that in these daungerous times,
I doo not like this frowning vulgare brow.

158. *let*] written *lets* and the *s* crossed out, though perhaps
only in modern ink.
    Sc. iii. This (as well as the intervening Sc. ii) is again part
of the original text in Munday's hand.
    1–8. Tilney has marked these lines in the margin and added
the note: 'Mend yis'.

My searching eye did neuer entertaine,
a more distracted countenaunce of greefe
then I haue late obseru'de
in the displeased commons of the Cittie.

Sur. Tis straunge, that from his princely clemencie,
    so well a tempred mercie and a grace,   10
    to all the aliens in this fruitefull land,
    that this highe-creasted insolence should spring,
    from them that breathe from his maiestick
        bountie,
    that fatned with the trafficque of our countrey:
    alreadie leape into his subiects face.

Pal. Yet Sherwin['s] hindred to commence his suite
    against de Bard, by the Ambassadour
    by supplication made vnto the King.
    Who hauing first entic'de away his wife,
    and gott his plate, neere woorth foure hundred
        pound,   20
    to greeue some wronged cittizens, that found,
    this vile disgrace oft cast into their teeth:
    of late sues Sherwin, and arrested him
    for monie for the boording of his wife.

Sur. The more knaue Bard, that vsing Sherwins
        goods,
    dooth aske him interest for the occupation:
    I like not that my Lord of Shrewesburie.
    Hees ill bested, that lends a well pac'de horsse,
    vnto a man that will not finde him meate.

Cholme. My Lord of Surrey will be pleasant still.   30

Pal. I beeing then imployed by your honors
    to stay the broyle that fell about the same,
    wher by perswasion I enforc'de the wrongs,
    and vrgde the greefe of the displeased Cittie:
    he answerd me and with a sollemne oathe

that if he had the Maior of Londons wife,
he would keepe her in despight of any Englishe.

Sur. Tis good Sir Thomas then for you and me,
your wife is dead, and I a batcheler
if no man can possesse his wife alone,   40
I am glad Sir Thomas Palmer I haue none.

Cholme. If a take my wife, a shall finde her meate.

Sur. And reason good (Sir Roger Cholmeley) too.
If these hott Frenchemen needsly will haue
    sporte,
they should in kindnesse yet deffraye the charge.
Tis hard when men possesse our wiues in quiet:
and yet leaue vs in to discharge their diett.

Shrew. My Lord, our catours shall not vse the markett,
for our prouision, but some straunger now:
will take the vittailes from him he hath bought. 50
A carpenter, as I was late enformde,
who hauing bought a paire of dooues in Cheape,
immediately a Frencheman tooke them from
    him,
and beat the poore man for resisting him.
And when the fellowe did complaine his
    wrongs:
he was seuerely punish'de for his labour.

Sur. But if the Englishe blood be once but vp,
as I perceiue theire harts alreadie full,
I feare me much, before their spleenes be
    coolde,
some of these saucie aliens for their pride,   60

37. Tilney has crossed out *Englishe* and substituted *mã*
49. Tilney has crossed out *straunger* and interlined *lombard*
53. Tilney has crossed out *Frencheman* and interlined *Lombard*
57–70, 73–8 (?) are marked for omission, probably by Tilney.

will pay for't soundly, wheresoere it lights.
This tyde of rage, that with the eddie striues:
I feare me much will drowne too manie liues.

Cholme. Now afore God, your honors, pardon me,
men of your place and greatnesse, are to
    blame,
I tell ye true my Lords, in that his Maiestie
is not informed of this base abuse,
and dayly wrongs are offered to his subiects
for if he were, I knowe his gracious wisedome,
would soone redresse it.   70

          Enter a Messenger

Shrew. Sirra, what newes?
Cholme. None good I feare.
Mess. My Lord, ill newes, and wursse I feare will
    followe
if speedily it be not lookte vnto.
The Cittie is in an vproare and the Maior,
is threatned if he come out of his house.
A number poore artifi[cers]...........
....
.........fearde what this would come vnto.   FOL. 5*b*

[   ] This followes on the doctours publishing
the bill of wrongs in publique at the Spittle.   80
Shrew. That doctor Beale may chaunce beshrewe him-
for reading of the bill.   [selfe
Pal. Let vs goe gather forces to the Maior,
for quick suppressing this rebellious route.
Sur. Now I bethinke myselfe of Maister Moore,
one of the Sheriffes, a wise and learned gentle-
    man,
and in especiall fauour with the people.
He backt with other graue and sober men,

           may by his gentle and perswasiue speeche
           perhaps preuaile more than we can with power. 90
Shrew.   Beleeue me, but your honor well aduises.
           Let vs make haste, or I doo greatly feare:
           some to their graues this mornings woorke will
              beare.   *Exeunt.*

     [SCENE IV. A Street in Saint Martin's-le-Grand.]

     Enter Lincolne, Betses, Williamson, Sherwin and
other armed, Doll in a shirt of maile, a head piece,
sword and buckler, a crewe attending.

Clo.   Come come wele tickle ther turnips wele Fᴏʟ. 7ᵃ
           butter ther boxes shall strangers rule the roste
           but wele baste the roste come come a flawnt
           a flaunte.
George.   Brother giue place and heare Iohn Lincolne
              speake.
Clo.   I Lincolne my leder and Doll my true breder
           with the rest of our crue shall Ran tan tarra
           ran · doo all they what they can shall we be
           bobd braude no shall we be hellde vnder no ·
           we ar fre borne and doo take skorne to be 10
           vsde soe.

     Sc. iv. This is a revised version written in hand B. The earlier version, part of the original text in Munday's hand, occupies the middle portion of fol. 5*b*. The revision differs little from the original except for the rather lamentable addition of the Clown's part. There is no initial direction in the revision; that printed above is taken from the original version, where it was left standing when the text that follows was deleted. But hand C has written in the margin the alternative direction: 'Enter Lincolne betts williamson Doll.' This ignores Sherwin, who is undoubtedly present in both versions, but who may nevertheless have been marked down for omission (see below, Sc. vi). Fol. 6 contains a revision of a later scene misplaced.

     6–11. Dyce prints this jingle as ten lines of verse.

Doll. Pease theare I saye heare captaine Lincolne
      speake.
      Kepe silens till we know his minde at large.
Clo. Then largelye dilliuer speake bullie and he that
      presumes to interrupte the in thie orratione this
      for him.
Lincol. Then gallant bloods you whoes fre sowles doo
      skorne
      to beare the inforsed wrongs of alians
      ad rage to ressolutione fier the howses
      of theis audatious strangers: This is Saint Martins 20
      and yonder dwells Mutas a welthy Piccarde
      at the Greene Gate
      de Barde Peter van Hollocke Adrian Martine
      with many more outlandishe fugetiues
      shall theis enioy more priueledge then wee
      in our owne cuntry · lets become ther slaiues
      since iustis kepes not them in greater awe
      wele be ourselues rough ministers at lawe.
Clo. Vse no more swords nor no more words but fier
      the howses braue captaine curragious fier me 30
      ther howses.
Doll. I for we maye as well make bonefiers on maye
      daye as at midsommer wele alter the daye in the
      callinder and sett itt downe in flaming letters.
Sher. Staye no that wold much indanger the hole cittie
      wher too I wold not the leaste preiudice.
Doll. No nor I nether so maie mine owne howse be
      burnd for companye Ile tell ye what wele drag
      the strangers into Morefeldes and theare bum-
      baste them till they stinke againe.   40

21. *mutas*] *t* altered from *l* probably by C.
Piccarde] so in the original version; miswritten *piccardye* in
revision.

Clo. And thats soone doone for they smell for feare
     all redye.

Geor. Let some of vs enter the strangers houses
     and if we finde them theare then bring them
       forthe.

Doll. But if ye bringe them forthe eare ye finde
     them Ile neare alowe of thatt.

Clo. Now Marsse for thie honner Dutch or
     Frenshe so yt be a wenshe Ile vppon hir.
                      Exeunt some and Sherwin.

William. Now lads howe shall we labor in our saftie
     I heare the maire hath gatherd men in armes 50
     and that shreue More an hower agoe risseude
     some of the privye cownsell in at Ludgate
     forse now must make our pease or eles we fall
     twill soone be knowne we ar the principall.

Doll. And what of that if thow beest afraide husband
     go home againe and hide thy hed for by the
     lord Ile haue a lyttill sporte now we ar att
     ytt.

Geor. Lets stand vppon our swords and if they come
     resseaue them as they weare our enemyes.   60
                 Enter Sherwin & the rest.

48. The direction has been supplied from the original version; there is none in the revision.

49. *Williā*] written by C over *Linco* of B; the speech has
the prefix *Will* in the original version, and Doll's reply puts the
attribution beyond question.

59. *Geor.*] B first wrote *Lin* again, but corrected it himself;
the original has *Geo.*

swords] original version *Guarde*, but the sense is 'rely on
our arms.'

60. *enemyes*] so in the original version; B wrote *eninemyes* but
the *i* is crossed out, though perhaps only in modern ink.

The direction has been supplied from the original version;
there is none in the revision.

Clo. A purchase a purchase we haue fownd we ha
    fownde.
Doll. What.
Clo. Nothinge nott a Frenshe Fleminge nor a
    Fleming Frenshe to be fownde but all fled in
    plaine Inglishe.
Linco. How now haue you fownd any.
Sher. No not one theyre all fled.
Lincol. Then fier the houses that the maior beinge
        busye
    aboute the quenshinge of them we maye skape 70
    burne downe ther kennells let vs straite awaye
    leaste this daye proue to vs an ill Maye daye.
Clo. Fier fier Ile be the firste
    if hanginge come tis welcome thats the worste.
                                    Exeunt.

[Scene V. The Guildhall.]

Enter at on dore Sir Thomas Moore and Lord Fol. 7*b*
Maire: att another doore Sir Iohn Munday hurt.

L. Maior. What Sir Iohn Munday are you hurt.

    74. The direction has again been supplied from the original
version. The revision has 'Manett Clowne', but this was added
in a different ink and hand, possibly by C, though it is not much
like his writing. It was evidently intended to carry the Clown
over to a revised version of the Prentice scene (see following
note).
    Sc. v. This scene, written in hand C, belongs to the revision,
where it follows immediately on the revised version of Sc. iv.
It is not certain whether or not it had any prototype in the
original text, but it seems most likely that it is entirely new and
intended to replace the original fifth scene, the beginning of
which is still extant following on the original version of Sc. iv
at the foot of fol. 5*b*. This fragment, in prose, presents a number
of Prentices playing at cudgels in Cheapside and no doubt included the wounding of Sir John Munday as related in the
revisional scene. See below, p. 226.

Sir Iohn. A little knock my lord ther was even now
a sort of prentises playing at cudgells
I did comaund them to ther maisters howses
but one of them backt by the other crew
wounded me in the forhead with his cudgill
and now I feare me they are gon to ioine
with Lincolne Sherwine and ther dangerous
traine.

Moore. The captaines of this insurection
have tane themselves to armes · and cam but
now   10
to both the counters wher they have releast
sundrie indetted prisoners · and from thence
I heere that they are gonn into Saint Martins
wher they intend to offer violence
to the amazed Lombards therfore my lord
if we expect the saftie of the Cittie
tis time that force or parley doe encownter
with thes displeased men.

Enter a Messenger.

L. maior. How now what newes.

Mess. My Lord the rebells have broake open
Newegate
from whence they have deliverd manie
prisoners   20
both fellons and notorious murderers
that desperatlie cleave to ther lawles traine.

L. Maior. Vpp with the draw bridge gather som forces
to Cornhill and Cheapside. And gentle men ·
If dilligence be vsde one every side
a quiet ebb will follow this rough tide.

Enter Shrowsberie Surrie Palmer · Cholmley.

1–8. Heavily marked for omission.

Shro. Lord Maior his maiestie receaving notice ·
       of this most dangerous insurection ·
       hath sent my Lord of Surry and myself
       Sir Thomas Palmer and our followers   30
       to add vnto [y]our forces our best meanes
       for pacifying of this mutinie
       In gods name then sett one with happie speed
       the king laments if one true subiect bleede.
Surr. I heere they meane to fier the Lumbards
            howses
       oh power what art thou in a madmans eies
       thou makst the plodding iddiott bloudy wise.
Moore. My Lords I dowt not but we shall appease
       with a calm breath this flux of discontent.
Palme. To call them to a parley questionles   40
       may fall out good · tis well said Maister
            Moore.
Moor. Letts to thes simple men for many sweat
       vnder this act that knowes not the lawes debtt
       which hangs vppon ther lives · for sillie men ·
       plodd on they know not how · like a fooles penn
       that ending showes not any sentence writt
       linckt but to common reason or sleightest witt
       thes follow for no harme but yett incurr
       self penaltie with those that raisd this stirr
       A gods name one to calme our privat foes   50
       with breath of gravitie not dangerous blowes.
                                    Exeunt.

44–7. Marked for omission, but a subsequent mark may be
intended to make the omission begin at l. 45 only. The last
four words of l. 45 are crossed out as well.

[SCENE VI. The Gate of Saint Martin's-le-Grand.]

Enter Lincoln · Doll · Clown · Georg Betts Williamson others and a Sergaunt at Armes.

Lincolne. Peace heare me, he that will not see a Fol. 8a
red hearing at a Harry grote, butter at
alevenpence a pounde, meale at nyne
shillings a bushell and beeff at fower
nobles a stone, lyst to me.

Geo. Bett. Yt will come to that passe yf straingers
be sufferd mark him.

Linco. Our countrie is a great eating country,
argo they eate more in our countrey then
they do in their owne.   10

Betts Clow. By a half penny loff a day troy waight.

Linc. They bring in straing rootes, which is
meerly to the vndoing of poor prentizes,
for whats a sorry parsnyp to a good hart.

William. Trash trash; they breed sore eyes and tis
enough to infect the Cytty with the palsey.

Sc. vi. The initial direction is written by C immediately
below the preceding scene. The next three pages of the manuscript, written by hand D (believed to be Shakespeare's),
contain the revision of the earlier and larger portion of a scene,
the end of which is preserved and left standing in the original
text. C has again omitted Sherwin's name from the direction,
and has likewise removed him from the text of the revision (see
ll. 35, 39 below): he is addressed in the original ending (l. 183)
though he has no part. This attempt to get rid of a minor but
still important character can only be due to difficulties of casting
and corroborates the evidence afforded by the occurrence of
Goodall's name (fol. 13*a) that the parts were actually
assigned.

6. *Geo bett*] substituted by C for *other* of D.
11. *betts clow*] substituted by C for *other* of D.
15. *william*] substituted by C for *oth* of D.

> *Lin.* Nay yt has infected yt with the palsey,
> for theise basterds of dung as you knowe
> they growe in dvng haue infected vs, and
> yt is our infeccion will make the Cytty 20
> shake which partly coms through the
> eating of parsnyps.

Clown · Betts. Trewe and pumpions togeather.

> *Seriant.* What say you to the mercy of the king
> do you refuse yt.

> *Lin.* You woold haue vs vppon thipp woold
> you no marry do we not, we accept of
> the kings mercy but wee will showe no
> mercy vppon the straingers.

> *Seriaunt.* You ar the simplest things that euer 30
> stood in such a question.

> *Lin.* How say you now prenty[sses] prentisses
> simple down with him.

> *All.* Prentisses symple prentisses symple.

*Enter the Lord Maier Surrey Shrewsbury [Palmer
Cholmeley Moore.]*

> *Maior.* Hold in the kings name hold.
> *Surrey.* Frends masters countrymen.
> *Mayer.* Peace how peace I charg you keep the
> peace.
> *Shro.* My masters countrymen.
> *Williamson.* The noble Earle of Shrewsbury letts
> hear him.   40

23. *Clown · betts*] substituted by C for *o* of D.
24. *Seriant*] C prefixed *Enter* but he had already brought
on the *sergaunt at armes* in his initial direction.
35. *maior*] substituted by C for *Sher*[*win*] of D, which is
clearly an error, perhaps for *Shre*[*wsbury*].
39. *williamson*] substituted by C for *Sher*[*win*] of D, which
was clearly intentional.

Ge. Betts. Weele heare the Earle of Surrey.

Linc. The Earle of Shrewsbury.

Betts. Weele heare both.

All. Both both both both.

Linc. Peace I say peace ar you men of wisdome
    or what ar you.

Surr. What you will haue them but not men
    of wisdome.

All. Weele not heare my Lord of Surrey, no
    no no no no Shrewsbury Shr[ewsbury].

Moor. Whiles they ar ore the banck of their
    obedyenc   50
    thus will they bere downe all things.

Linc. Shreiff Moor speakes shall we heare
    Shreef Moor speake.

Doll. Letts heare him a keepes a plentyfull
    shrevaltry, and a made my brother
    Arther Watchins Seriant Safes yeoman
    lets heare Shreeve Moore.

All. Shreiue Moor Moor More Shreue Moore.

Moor. Even by the rule you haue among your ᶠᵒʟ. ⁸ᵇ
    sealues
    comand still audience.   60

All. Surrey Sury.

All. Moor Moor.

Lincolne Betts. Peace peace scilens peace.

Moor. You that haue voyce and credyt with
    the nvmber
    comaund them to a stilnes.

Lincolne. A plaigue on them they will not hold
    their peace
    the deule cannot rule them.

41. *Ge*] prefixed by C.

66–7. These lines are divided after *deule* in the manuscript.

Moor. Then what a rough and ryotous charge haue you
      to leade those that the deule cannot rule
      good masters heare me speake.   70
 Doll. I byth mas will we Moor thart a good hows-
      keeper and I thanck thy good worship for my
      brother Arthur Watchins.
  All. Peace peace.
Moor. Look what you do offend you cry vppon
      that is the peace; not [on] of you heare present
      had there such fellowes lyvd when you wer babes
      that coold haue topt the peace, as nowe you woold
      the peace wherin you haue till nowe growne vp
      had bin tane from you, and the bloody tymes 80
      coold not haue brought you to the state of men
      alas poor things what is yt you haue gott
      although we graunt you geat the thing you seeke.
 Bett. Marry the removing of the straingers which
      cannot choose but much advauntage the poor
      handycraftes of the Cytty.
Moor. Graunt them remoued and graunt that this your
          noyce
      hath chidd downe all the maiestie of Ingland
      ymagin that you see the wretched straingers
      their babyes at their backs, with their poor lugage 90
      plodding tooth ports and costs for transportacion
      and that you sytt as kings in your desyres
      aucthoryty quyte sylenct by your braule
      and you in ruff of your opynions clothd
      what had you gott; Ile tell you, you had taught
      how insolenc and strong hand shoold prevayle
      how ordere shoold be quelld, and by this patterne
      not on of you shoold lyve an aged man
      for other ruffians as their fancies wrought

    88. *maiestie*] D wrote *matie* without contraction mark.

with sealf same hand sealf reasons and sealf right 100
woold shark on you and men lyke revenous
    fishes
woold feed on on another.

Doll. Before god thats as trewe as the gospell.

Lincoln. Nay this a sound fellowe I tell you lets mark
    him.

Moor. Let me sett vp before your thoughts good freinds
on supposytion, which if you will marke
you shall perceaue howe horrible a shape
your ynnovation beres, first tis a sinn
which oft thappostle did forwarne vs of   110
vrging obedienc to aucthoryty
and twere no error yf I told you all
you wer in armes gainst g[od].

All. Marry god forbid that.   FOL. 9a

Moo. Nay certainly you ar
for to the king god hath his offyc lent
of dread of iustyce, power and comaund
hath bid him rule, and willd you to obay
and to add ampler maiestie to this
he hath not only lent the king his figure   120
his throne and sword, but gyven him his owne
    name
calls him a god on earth, what do you then
rysing gainst him that god himsealf enstalls
but ryse gainst god, what do you to your sowles
in doing this o desperat as you are ·

102. It is impossible to be certain whether D intended 'on
one another' or 'one on another.'

104. lincoln] substituted by C for Betts of D.

106. moor] supplied by C.

110–1, 112–3. Each pair is written as one line by D, thus
completing the speech on the page.

wash your foule mynds with teares and those
    same hands
that you lyke rebells lyft against the peace
lift vp for peace, and your vnreuerent knees
make them your feet to kneele to be for-
    gyven;
tell me but this what rebell captaine   130
as mutynes ar incident, by his name
can still the rout who will obay a traytor
or howe can well that proclamation sounde
when ther is no adicion but a rebell
to quallyfy a rebell, youle put downe straingers
kill them cutt their throts possesse their howses
and leade the maiestie of law in liom
to slipp him lyke a hound; say nowe the king
as he is clement, yf thoffendor moorne
shoold so much com to short of your great
    trespas   140
as but to banysh you, whether woold you go ·
what country by the nature of your error
shoold gyve you harber go you to Fraunc or
    Flanders
to any Iarman province, Spane or Portigall
nay any where that not adheres to Ingland
why you must needs be straingers, woold you
    be pleasd
to find a nation of such barbarous temper
that breaking out in hiddious violence
woold not afoord you, an abode on earth
whett their detested knyves against your throtes 150
spurne you lyke doggs, and lyke as yf that god

130. *tell me but this*] Before these words, interlined by C,
the equivalent of three lines has been crossed out by the same.
137. *maiestie*] D wrote *matie* without contraction mark.

owed not nor made not you, nor that the
    elaments
wer not all appropriat to your comforts ·
but charterd vnto them, what woold you thinck
to be thus vsd, this is the straingers case
and this your momtanish inhumanyty.

All. Fayth a saies trewe letts do as wc may be
    doon by.

Linco. Weele be ruld by you Master Moor yf youle
    stand our freind to procure our pardon   160

Moor. Submyt you to theise noble gentlemen
    entreate their mediation to the kinge
    gyve vp yoursealf to forme obay the maiestrate
    and thers no doubt, but mercy may be found
    yf you so seek [yt].

All. We yeeld, and desire his highnesse mercie.   Fol. 10a
               They lay by their weapons.

Moore. No doubt his maiestie will graunt it you
    but you must yeeld to goe to seuerall prisons,
    till that this highnesse will be further knowne.

All. Moste willingly, whether you will haue vs.   170

Shrew. Lord Maior, let them be sent to seuerall
    prisons,

156. *momtanish*] None of the proposed emendations, *mount-anish, mawmtanish, moritanish,* is at all satisfactory.

157. D wrote *letts vs* and *vs* was crossed out, probably by C.

159. *Linco*] substituted by C for *all* repeated by D.

164–5. Written as one line by D in order to complete his revision on the page.

Fol. 9*b* is blank. The scene is continued in its original form and in Munday's hand on fol. 10*a*. There is a slight overlap, for the first three lines of the page (marked for omission) contain the end of More's original speech. They are in prose and run: 'To persist in it, is present death · but if you yeeld yourselues, no doubt, what punishment you (in simplicitie[)] haue incurred, his highnesse in mercie will moste graciously pardon.'

and there in any case, be well intreated.
My Lord of Surrie, please you to take
    horsse,
and ride to Cheapeside, where the Aldermen,
are with their seuerall companies in armes.
Will them to goe vnto their seuerall wardes,
bothe for the stay of further mutinie,
and for the apprehending of such persons:
as shall contend.

Sur. I goe my noble Lord.   *Exit Surrey.*

Shrew. weele straite goe tell his highnesse these good
    newes.   180
    Withall (Shreeue Moore) Ile tell him, how
      your breath:
    hath ransomde many a subiect from sad death.
             Exeunt Shrewsbury and Cholmeley.

L. Maior. Lincolne and Sherwine, you shall bothe to
    Newgate,
    the rest vnto the Counters.

Pal. Goe, guarde them hence, a little breath well
    spent,
    cheates expectation in his fairst euent.

Doll. Well Sheriffe Moore, thou hast doone more
    with thy good woordes, then all they could
    with their weapons: giue me thy hand, keepe
    thy promise now for the Kings pardon, or by 190
    the Lord Ile call thee a plaine conie catcher.

Lin. Farewell Shreeue Moore, and as we yeeld
    by thee
    so make our peace, then thou dealst honestly.

Clo. I and saue vs from the gallowes eles a deales
    dobble.   *They are led away.*

194–5. The Clown's speech is added by B in the margin.

L. Maior. Maister Shreeue Moore, you haue pre-
        seru'de the Cittie,
        from a moste daungerous fierce commotion.
        For if this limbe of riot heere in Saint
           Martins,
        had ioynd with other braunches of the Cittie,
        that did begin to kindle, twould haue bred, 200
        great rage, that rage, much murder would
           haue fed.
Moore. My Lord, and bretheren, what I heere haue
        spoke,
        my countries looue, and next, the Citties
        care:
        enioynde me to, which since it thus pre-
           uailes,
        thinke, God hath made weake Moore his
           instrument,
        to thwart seditions violent intent.
        I thinke twere best my Lord, some two
           houres hence,
        we meete at the Guildehall, and there de-
           termine,
        that thorow euery warde, the watche be clad
        in armour, but especially prouide   210
        that at the Cittie gates, selected men,
        substantiall cittizens doo warde tonight,
        for feare of further mischeife.
L. Maior. It shall be so.

              Enter Shrewsbury.

   201. After this two lines are marked for omission, the first
assigned to *Pal*[*mer*], and the second to *Sh*[*rewsbury*], who
left the stage l. 182, whence the deletion. They run: 'not Steele
but eloquence hath wrought this good. | you haue redeemde vs
from much threatned blood.'

But yond me thinks my Lord of Shrewesburie.

Shrew. My Lord, his maiestie sends loouing thankes,
 to you, your bretheren, and his faithfull
  subiects
 your carefull cittizens. But Maister Moore,
  to you,
 a rougher, yet as kinde a salutation,
 your name is yet too short, nay, you must
  kneele,
 a knights creation is thys knightly steele. 220
 Rise vp Sir Thomas Moore.

Moore. I thanke his highnesse for thus honoring me.

Shrew. This is but first taste of his princely fauour,
 for it hath pleased his high maiestie,
 (noating your wisedome and deseruing
  meritt,)
 to put this staffe of honor in your hand,
 for he hath chose you of his Priuie Councell.

Moore. My Lord, for to denye my Soueraignes
  bountie,
 were to drop precious stones into the heapes
 whence first they came, 230
 to vrdge my imperfections in excuse,
 were all as stale as custome. No my Lord,
 my seruice is my Kings, good reason why:
 since life and death hangs on our Soueraignes
  eye.

L. Maior. His maiestie hath honord much the Cittie
 in this his princely choise.

Moore. My Lord and bretheren,
 though I departe for......my looue shall rest

230. The second half of this line 'from whence they'd nere
returne,' has been crossed out with good reason.

....

I now must sleepe in courte, sounde sleepes Fol. 10*b*
    forbeare,
the chamberlain to state is publique care.   240
Yet in this rising of my priuate blood:
my studious thoughts shall tend the Citties
    good.
Enter Croftes.

Shrew. How now Croftes? what newes?
Croftes. My Lord, his highnesse sends expresse com-
    maunde,
that a record be entred of this riott,
and that the cheefe and capitall offendours
be theron straite arraignde, for himselfe intends
to sit in person on the rest to morrowe
at Westminster.
Shrew. Lord Maior, you heare your charge.
Come good Sir Thomas Moore, to court let's
    hye   250
you are th'appeaser of this mutinie.
Moore. My Lord farewell, new dayes begets new tides
life whirles bout fate, then to a graue it slydes.
Exeunt seuerally.

[Scene VII. Cheapside.]
Enter Maister Sheriffe, and meete a Messenger.

Sheriff. Messenger, what newes?
Mess. Is execution yet performde?
Sheriff. Not yet, the cartes stand readie at the stayres,
and they shall presently away to Tibourne.
Messe. Stay Maister Shreeue, it is the Councelles
    pleasure,

Sc. vii. Part of the original text in Munday's hand.

for more example in so bad a case,
a Iibbit be erected in Cheapside,
hard by the standerd, whether you must bring
Lincolne, and those that were the cheefe with
    him,
to suffer death, and that immediatly.   10

Enter Officers.

Sheriff. It shalbe doone Sir. (*exit Messenger.*) Officers,
    be speedie
call for a Iibbit, see it be erected,
others make haste to Newgate, bid them bring,
the prisoners hether, for they heere must dye,
Away I say, and see no time be slackt.
Off. We goe Sir.
Sheriff. Thats well said fellowes, now you doo your
    dutie.

Exeunt some seuerally, others set vp the Iibbit.

God for his pittie help these troublous times.
The streetes stopte vp with gazing multitudes,
commaund our armed officers with halberds, 20
make way for entraunce of the prisoners.
Let proclamation once againe be made,
that euery housholder, on paine of deathe
keep in his prentises, and euery man,
stand with a weapon readie at his doore,
as he will answere to the contrary.
Off. Ile see it doone Sir.   *Exit.*

Enter another Officer.

Sheriffe. Bring them away to execution,
the writt is come abooue two houres since,
the Cittie will be fynde for this neglect.   30

17–30. Marked for omission.

Off. Thers such a preasse and multitude at New-
      gate,
    they cannot bring the cartes vnto the stayres
    to take the prisoners in.
Sheriff. Then let them come on foote,
    we may not dally time with great commaund.
Off. Some of the Benche Sir, thinke it very fit
    that stay be made, and giue it out abroade
    the execution is deferd till morning,
    and when the streetes shall be a little cleerd,
    to chaine them vp, and suddenly dispatch it.
Sheriff. Stay, in meane time me thinkes they come
    along.   40

    The Prisoners are brought in well guarded.

    See, they are comming, so, tis very well.
    Bring Lincolne there the first vnto the tree.
Clo. I for I cry lag Sir.
Lin. I knewe the first Sir, did belong to me.
    This the olde prouerbe now compleate dooth
        make,
    that Lincolne should be hangd for Londons
        sake.
    A Gods name, lets to woorke: (*he goes vp.*)
        fellowe, dispatche,
    I was the formoste man in this rebellion
    and I the formoste that must dye for it.
Doll. Brauely Iohn Lincolne, let thy death expresse, 50
    that as thou liu'dst a man, thou dyedst no lesse.
Lin. Doll Williamson, thine eyes shall witnesse it.
    Then to all you that come to viewe mine end,
    I must confesse, I had no ill intent,
    but against such as wrongd vs ouer much.

43. Added by B in the margin.

And now I can perceiue, it was not fit,
that priuate men should carue out their re-
    dresse,
which way they list, no, learne it now by me
obedience is the best in eche degree.
And asking mercie meekely of my King,   60
I paciently submit me to the lawe.
But God forgiue them that were cause of it ·
and as a Christian, truely from my hart:
I likewise craue they would forgiue me too.
....
that others by example of the same   FOL. 11*a*
hencefoorth be warned to attempt the like
gainst any alien that repaireth hether
fare ye well all, the next time that we meete
I trust in heauen we shall eche other greete. 70
                        He leapes off.

Doll. Farewell Iohn Lincoln, say all what they can:
       thou liu'dst a good fellowe, and dyedst an
           honest man.
Clo.   Wold I weare so farre on my iurney the first
       stretche is the worste me thinks.
Sheriff. Bring Williamson there forwarde.
Doll. Good Maister Shreeue, I haue an earnest
           suite,
       and as you are a man deny't me not.
Sheriff. Woman, what is it? be it in my power,
       thou shalt obtayne it.
Doll. Let me dye next Sir, that is all I craue,   80
       you knowe not what a comforte you shall
           bring
       to my poore hart to dye before my husband.
Sheriff. Bring her to death, she shall haue her desire.
       73–4. Added by B in the margin.

Clo. Sir and I haue a suite to you too.

[*Sheriff.*] What is ytt.

[*Clo.*] That as you haue hangd Lincolne first and will
    hange hir nexte so you will nott hange me at
    all.

[*Sheriff.*] Naye you set ope the counter gates and you
    must hange [for] the folye.   90

[*Clo.*] Well then so much for that.

Doll. Sir, your free bountie much contents my
    minde,
    commend me to that good Shreeue Maister
    Moore,
    and tell him had't not bin for his perswasion,
    Iohn Lincolne had not hung heere as he does ·
    we would first haue [bin] lockt vp in Leaden-
    hall,
    and there bin burnt to ashes with the roofe.

Sheriff. Woman, what Maister Moore did, was a
    subiects dutie,
    and hath so pleasde our gracious Lord the
    King,
    that he is hence remoou'de to higher place,   100
    and made of Councell to his Maiestie.

Doll. Well is he woorthie of it by my troth,
    an honest, wise, well spoken gentleman,
    yet would I praise his honestie much more,
    if he had kept his woord, and sau'de our liues,
    but let that passe, men are but men, and so,
    woords are but wordes, and payes not what
    men owe.
    Now husband, since perhaps the world may
    say,

84-91. Added by B in the margin, the first speaker only
being indicated.

that through my meanes thou comste thus to
    thy end:
heere I beginne this cuppe of death to thee,   110
because thou shalt be sure to taste no wursse,
then I haue taken, that must goe before thee.
What though I be a woman, thats no matter,
I doo owe God a death, and I must pay him.
Husband, giue me thy hand, be not dismayed,
this charre beeing charde, then all our debt is
    payd.
Only two little babes we leaue behinde vs,
and all I can bequeathe them at this time,
is but the looue of some good honest freend:
to bring them vp in charitable sorte.   120
What maisters, he goes vpright that neuer
    haltes,
and they may liue to mend their parents faultes.

Will. Why well sayd wife, yfaith thou cheerst my
    hart,
giue me thy hand, lets kisse, and so lets part.
                    He kisses her on the ladder.

Doll. The next kisse Williamson, shalbe in heauen.
Now cheerely lads, George Bets, a hand with
    thee,
and thine too Rafe, and thine good honest
    Sherwin.
Now let me tell the women of this towne,
No straunger yet brought Doll to lying downe.
So long as I an Englishman can see,   130
Nor Frenche nor Dutche shall get a kisse of
    me.
And when that I am dead, for me yet say,
I dyed in scorne to be a straungers preye.
                    A great shout and noise.

(*within.*) Pardon, pardon, pardon, pardon
    roome for the Ea[r]le of Surrey, roome there
    roome.

Enter Surrey.

Sur. Saue the mans life, if it be possible.

Sheriff. It is too late my Lord, hees dead alreadie.

Sur. I tell ye Maister Sheriffe, you are too forwarde,
    to make such haste with men vnto their death,
    I thinke your paines will merit little thankes 140
    since that his highnesse is so mercifull,
    as not to spill the blood of any subiect.

Sheriff. My noble Lord, would we so much had
    knowen,
    the Councelles warrant hastened our dispatche,
    it had not else bin doone so suddenly.

Sur. Sir Thomas Moore humbly vppon his knee,
    did begge the liues of all, since on his woord
    they did so gently yeeld. The King hath
    graunted it,
    and made him Lord High Chauncellour of
    England,
    according as he woorthily deserues.   150
    Since Lincolnes life cannot be had againe,
    then for the rest, from my dread Soueraignes
    lippes,
    I heere pronounce free pardon for them all.

All (*flinging vp cappes*). God saue the King, God
    saue the King,
    my good Lord Chauncellour and the Earle of
    Surrey.

Doll. And doll desires it from her very hart,
    Moores name may liue for this right noble
    part.

And whensoere we talke of ill May day:
praise Moore [whose]................................ 159
Sur. In hope his highnesse clemencie and mercie,   Fol. 11*b*
which in the armes of milde and meeke compassion
would rather clip you, as the loouing nursse
oft dooth the waywarde infant, then to leaue you,
to the sharp rodd of iustice so to drawe you,
to shun such lewde assemblies, as beget
vnlawfull riots and such trayterous acts,
that striking with the hand of priuate hate,
maime your deare countrie with a publique wounde.
Oh God, that mercie, whose maiestick browe,
should be vnwrinckled, and that awefull iustice,   170
which looketh through a vaile of sufferaunce
vppon the frailtie of the multitude
should with the clamours of outragious wrongs,
be stird and wakened thus to punishment.
But your deserued death he dooth forgiue,
who giues you life, pray all he long may liue.
All. God saue the King, God saue the King,
my good Lord Chauncellour and the Earle of
Surrey.   *Exeunt.*

[The End.]

170–4. Marked for omission. It is not obvious why these
fine lines should have been condemned.

APPENDIX

[The following is the beginning of the original fifth
scene, between the Prentices in Cheapside, as preserved in
Munday's hand at the foot of fol. 5*b*. It is marked for
omission and was cancelled altogether in revision, the scene
at the Guildhall being presumably substituted in its place.]

*Enter three or foure Prentises of trades, with a paire
of cudgelles.*

Harry. Come, lay downe the cudgelles.—Hoh Robin,
    you met vs well at Bunhill, to haue you with vs
    a Mayng this morning?
Robin. Faith Harrie, the head drawer at the Miter by
    the great conduite, calld me vp, and we went to
    breakefast into Saint Annes lane. But come,
    who beginnes? In good faith I am cleane out of
    practise: when wast at Garrets schoole Harrie?
Har. Not this great while, neuer since I brake his
    vshers head, when he plaid his schollers prize at 10
    the Starre in Bread streete, I vse all to George
    Philpots at Dowgate, hees the best backsworde
    man in England.
Kit. Bate me an ace of that, quoth Bolton.
Har. Ile not bate ye a pinne on't Sir, for, by this
    cudgell tis true.
Kit. I will cudgell that oppinion out of ye: did you
    breake an vshers head Sir?
Har. I marie did I Sir.
Kit. I am very glad on't, you shall breake mine too 20
    and ye can.

Har. Sirra, I pre thee what art thou?
  Kit. Why, I am a prentise as thou art, seest thou now:
        Ile play with thee at blunt heere in Cheapeside,
        and when thou hast doone, if thou beest angrie,
        Ile fight with thee at [sharp] in Moorefeildes
        I haue a swoord to serue my turne in a fauor...
        ....
        come Iulie, to serue ....
        30

VII. SPECIAL TRANSCRIPT
OF THE THREE PAGES

THE three pages of the Harleian manuscript written in hand D have twice already been reproduced in type-facsimile, first as part of the Malone Society's edition of the play (M), and later in Sir Edward Maunde Thompson's book on *Shakespeare's Handwriting* (T). In making yet another essay faithfully to interpret the sometimes obscure original for the use of modern readers, I have, of course, availed myself to the full of previous attempts. If the three prints are compared they will be found to differ in a number of details, which fall into several distinct groups. (i) Sir Edward's minute study of the manuscript, and the fact that, at his suggestion, the second page was relieved of its covering of tracing-paper, enabled him to correct certain happily small errors of M. These corrections were silently made and have been silently incorporated in the present text. (ii) I have also in general followed T in those details of capitalization and punctuation which must be classed as matters of opinion. (iii) Further, I have gladly availed myself of the readings of T in passages which were marked as indecipherable in M, though a fresh examination of the original has not always enabled me to distinguish quite as much as Sir Edward, and I have felt bound to record an occasional doubt in the notes. (iv) There are a few un-questionable errors (one serious) common to M and T, which I have, of course, taken the opportunity of correcting, at the same time as (v) two or three trifling slips in T, though in no case have I ventured to depart from Sir Edward's readings without recording the fact in the notes. (vi) Lastly there are two important readings which, since they cannot be conveniently dealt with in the foot-notes, are reserved for separate consideration at the end.

The few words or letters that have been irretrievably lost

or yet remain undeciphered have been supplied conjecturally within brackets. In doing so Dyce's readings, in so far
as he purported to be reproducing the original, have been
adopted, though it must be admitted that the minuter examination of the obscurities now possible rather tends to
shake one's confidence in his powers of decipherment.

I have aimed at preserving, so far as is possible in type,
the arrangement and general appearance of the original.
All words written by a hand other than D (in every case I
believe by C) are distinguished by heavier type. Where
deletions occur in conjunction with these insertions they
are to be taken as the work of the same corrector: all other
deletions are by D unless the contrary is stated in the notes.

It may be well to add that the present text has been
printed from an independent transcript made from the
excellent facsimiles in Sir Edward's book, so far as these
are legible, and carefully collated with M and T, while on
every point of possible doubt the original at the British
Museum has been examined.

The author wrote the text, at any rate of the first two
pages, continuously, dividing the speeches by rules but
without indicating the speakers. He then read it through,
inserting the prefixes and at the same time making certain
additions to the text, namely, some words at the beginning
of l. 22, at the end of l. 38, and the whole of l. 45. The
most natural explanation of the crowding of the text at the
foot of the second page is that the writer had no more paper
at hand, and that the third page was composed on a subsequent occasion; a supposition borne out by a marked
difference in the general style of the handwriting. The
addition of the speakers' names was certainly perfunctory,
especially on the first page, but, apart from the unsatisfactory
condition of the deleted passage on the third, I do not find
any evidence of haste or carelessness in the composition.

Lincolne	Peace heare me, he that will not ſee [a red] hearing at a harry grote, butter at a levenpence a pou[nde, meale at] nyne ſhillingꝭ a Buſhell and Beeff at fower nob[les a ſtone, lyꝛ]t to me
~~other~~ Geo bett	yt will Come to that paſſe yf ſtrain[gers be ſu]ffred mark him
Linco	our Countrie is a great eating Country, argo they eate more in our Countrey then they do in their owne 5
~~other~~ betts clow	by a half penny loſſ a day troy waight
Linc	they bring in ſtraing rootes, which is meerly to the vndoing of poor prentizes, for whatꝭ ~~a watrie~~ a ſorry pſnyp to a good hart
~~oth~~ william	traſh traſh, : they breed fore eyes and tis enough to infect the Cytty wt the palſey 10
Lin	nay yt has infected yt wt the palſey, for theiſe baſterdꝭ of dung as you knowe they growe in Dvng haue infected vs, and yt is our infeccion will make the Cytty ſhake which ꝑtly Coms through the eating of pſnyps 15

☙ **Clown · betts**   trewe and pumpions togeather
Enter
ſeriant

what ſay youᵘ to the mercy of the king do youᵘ refuſe yt

Lin

youᵘ woold haue[vs] vppon thipp woold youᵘ no marry dowenot, we
accept of the kingſ mercy but wee will ſhowe no mercy vppõ
the ſtraingers

20

ſeriaunt   youᵘ ar the ſimpleſt thingſ that eũ ſtood in ſuch a queſtion

now prenty

Lin   how ſay youᵘ prentiſſes ſymple downe wᵗʰ him

---

3 *Beeff*] the firſt *e* has been altered from some other letter.   5 *Linco*] *in* has two minims only but the
first is dotted.   8 *of*] the final curl of the *f* has been carried round in such a way as to resemble *o*
a semi-colon.   *traſh;*] so T, but the lower dot may be accidental: M prints
traſh,;] so T, but the lower dot may be accidental: M prints
10 *william*] *m* has two minims only.   12 *dung*] *un* has five minims.   17 The initial letter of the speaker's name,
whether it be regarded as minuscule (T) or majuscule (M), is certainly of an Italian type.   18 *haue*]
T *have* perhaps by an accidental slip; the word occurs elsewhere eight times always spelt *haue*, Dyce read
haue here, and the very obscure original seems to me to have *u* rather than *v*   19 *ſhowe*] *w* blotted,
possibly altered.   22 The marginal and interlined words were added later.   *prenty*] *n* is represented
by one minim only, and *y* is doubtful.

all	prentiſes ſymple prentiſes ſymple
	Enter the L. maier Surrey *Shrewſbury*
~~Sher~~ Maior	hold in the kingẻ name hold
Surrey	frendẻ maſters Countrymen
mayer	peace how peace J ꜰ Charg yoᵘ keep the peace
Shro·	my maſters Countrymen
~~Sher~~ Williamson	The noble Earle of Shrewſbury lettẻ hear him
Ge bettẻ	weele heare the Earle of Surrey
Linc	the earle of Shrewſbury
bettẻ	weele heare both
all	both both both both

25

30

Linc   Peace J ſay peace ar you^u men of Widome #̶ or
      what ar you^u

Surr   B̶u̶t̶ what you^u will haue them but not men of widome

all   weele not heare my L of Surrey, a̶l̶l̶ no no no no no
                           Shrewſbury ſhr

moor   whiles they ar ore the banck of their obedyenc   40
      thus will they bere downe all thing℮

Linc   Shreiff moor ſpeakes ſhall we heare ſhreef moor ſpeake

Doll   Lett℮ heare him a keepes a plentyfull ſhrevaltry, and a made my

26 *Sher*] this must be a slip for *Shre*   27 The rule has been accidentally omitted after this line.   29 *Shro·*] the last letter certainly seems to be *o* but D always writes *Shrewſbury* elsewhere.   30 C wrote his alteration on the top of D's original.   30, 32 *Shrewſbury*] M, T *Shrowsbury*   38 *all no... ſhr*] added later; the deletion is indistinguishable.   *Shrewſbury*] so M: T *Shrowsbury* (the letter is indistinguishable).   40 *thing℮*] I am unable to read the end of this word.   42 *ſhrevaltry,*] so M: T *shrevaltry.* but it is clearly a comma I think.

Brother Arther watchin[s] Seriant Safes yeoman let℮ heare
ſhreeve moore

all   Shreiue moor moor more Shreue moore

moor   [ev]en by the rule yo^u haue among yor fealues
Comand ſtill audience

all   [S]urrey Sury

all   moor moor

Lincolne bett℮   peace peace ſcilens peace

moor   Yo^u that haue voyce and Credyt w^t the ~~mv~~ nvmber
Comaund them to a ſtilnes

Lincolne   a plaigue on them they will not hold their peace the deule
Cannot rule them

moor   Then what a rough and ryotous charge haue yo^u

Doll

to Leade thofe that the deule Cannot rule
good mafters heare me fpeake

J byth mas will we moor thart a good howfkeeper and J
thanck thy good worfhip for my Brother Arthur watchins   60

all

peace peace

moor

look what yo^u do offend yo^u Cry vppō
that is the peace; not [on] of yo^u heare prefent
had there fuch fellowes lyvd when yo^u wer babes
that coold haue topt the peace, as nowe yo^u woold
the peace wherin yo^u haue till nowe growne vp
had bin tane from yo^u, and the bloody tymes
coold not haue brought yo^u to ~~theife~~ the ftate of men   65
alas poor thinge what is yt yo^u haue gott
although we graunt yo^u geat the thing yo^u feeke

43 *Safes*] *af* seems to me to have disappeared entirely except perhaps for the extreme tail of the *f*.   45 This line with the rule above it
yeoman] *o* altered, probably by C, from some other small letter.   was added later.   59 *watchins*] *c* altered, apparently from the beginning of *h*

D̶ Bett

marry the removing of the straingers wᶜʰ cannot choose but
much h̶e̶l̶p̶e̶ advauntage the poor handycraftes of the Cytty

70

moor

graunt them remoued and graunt that this yoʳ ẏ noyce
hath Chidd downe all the matie of Jngland
ymagin that yoᵘ see the wretched straingers

75

wᵗ
their babyes at their backℓ, a̶n̶d̶ their poor luggage
plodding tooth portℓ and costℓ for transportacion
and that yoᵘ sytt as kingℓ in your desyres
aucthoryty quyte sylenct by yoʳ braule
and yoᵘ in ruff of yoʳ t̶o̶ opynions clothd
what had yoᵘ gott; Jle tell yoᵘ, yoᵘ had taught
how insolenc and strong hand shoold prevayle

80

how orderd shoold be quelld, and by this patterne
not on of yoᵘ shoold lyve an aged man
for other ruffians as their fancies wrought
wᵗʰ sealf same hand sealf reasons and sealf right

85

woold shark on yoᵘ and men lyke ravenous fishes

Doll

woold feed on on another

Bette lincoln

before god thate as trewe as the gofpell

nay this a found fellowe J tell you lets mark him

moor

Let me fett vp before yor thoughts good freinde
on fuppofytion, which if you will marke
you fhall pceaue howe horrible a fhape
your ynnovation beres, firft tis a finn
which oft thappoftle did forwarne vs of vrging obedienc to aucthory[ty]
and twere itt no error yf J told you all   you wer in armes gainft g[od] 95

90

70 The *D* appears to have been crossed out by both D and C.   71 *handycraftes*] the *e* is represented
only by a small blot between *t* and *s*   72 *noyce*]*y* altered from *w*   73 *matie*] sic, by a slip
from *matie* i.e. *maieftie* (cf. l. 121).   75 *and* was crossed out, and *wt* interlined to replace it, by D.
Neither M nor T notices the alteration.   80 *gotts;*] so T: M prints a comma, but the original seems
to have ;.   82 *orderd*] so T: M *ordere* : doubtful, but in either case an error for *order*
85 *hand*] there is a very small dot after this word, some stop may possibly be intended.   89 *lincoln*] so M:
T *Lincoln* (perhaps a slip).   93 *your*] M, T *yor* but the reading though indistinct is hardly open
to question.   94 *vrging*] so M: T *vrging* (an accidental slip).

100

105

110

all

moo

marry god forbid that

nay certainly yoᵘ ar
for to the king god hath his offyc lent
of dread of Juftyce, power and Comaund
hath bid him rule, and willd yoᵘ to obay
and to add ampler maͤie to this
he ~~god~~ hath not ~~te~~ only lent the king his figure
&
his throne ~~his~~ fword, but gyven him his owne name
calls him a god on earth, what do yoᵘ then
ryfing gainft him that god himfealf enftalls
but ryfe gainft god, what do yoᵘ to yoʳ fowles
in doing this o defperat ~~ar~~ as you are•
wafh your foule mynds wᵗ teares and thofe fame handͤ
that yoᵘ lyke rebells lyft againft the peace
lift vp for peace, and your vnreuerent knees
~~that~~ make them your feet to kneele to be forgyven
~~is fafer warrs, then euer yoᵘ can make~~

in in to yor obediene.

whose discipline is ryot; why euen yor warrs hurly

tell me but this

cannot peeed but by obediene what rebell captaine

n

as mutyes ar incident, by his name

can fill the rout who will obay th a traytor

or howe can well that pclamation founde

when ther is no adicion but a rebell

to quallyfy a rebell, youle put downe ftraingers

115

101 *and*] *n* has three minims.   102 *only*] so M: T *souly* (withdrawn; see above, p. 76, note).
103 *his* (deleted)] so M: T *hys* (withdrawn; see above, p. 76, note). The & is really written on the top of *his*
not between the lines.   110 *and*] for an attempted alteration see final note.   111 There is a slightly
wider space after *feet* and a break may have been intended as in l. 95.   *to kneele*] so M: T *fo kneele* (an
accidental misprint due to a broken letter).   112–4 With the exception of the single word *warrs* (which
he crossed out, adding *hurly* in its place) these lines were left standing by D. All the other deletions are in
darker ink, presumably by C, who added the interlined words in the third line.   113 *warrs*] so
M: T *warre* altered to *warrs* (see final note).   *obedienc·*] T omits the stop, but I do not think that
the mark can be accidental.   117 *founde*] *un* has three minims.   118 *ther*] *r* altered from *ir*.

kill them cutt their throts poffeffe their howfes
and leade the matie of lawe in liom

~~alas alas~~

to flipp him lyke a hound; ~~fayeng~~ fay nowe the king
as he is clement, yf thoffendor moorne
fhoold fo much com to fhort of your great trefpas
as but to banyfh you, whether woold you go.
what Country by the nature of yor error
fhoold gyve you harber go you to ffraunc or flanders
to any Jarman pvince, ~~to~~ fpane or portigall
nay any where ~~why you~~ that not adheres to Jngland
why you muft needҿ be ftraingers, woold you be pleafd
to find a nation of fuch barbarous temper
that breaking out in hiddious violence
woold not afoord you, an abode on earth
whett their detefted knyves againft yor throtes
fpurne you lyke doggҿ, and lyke as yf that god
owed not nor made not you, nor that the elamentҿ

120

125

130

135

yᵒʳ

wcr not all appropriat to ~~their~~ Comfort(.
but Charterd vnto them, what woold you thinck
to be thus vfd, this is the ftraingers cafe
and this your momtanifh inhumanyty

---

fayth a faies trewe letts ~~vs~~ do as we may be doon by

121 *matie*] contraction mark omitted as in l. 73. 122 *fayeng*] M, T *saying* but there is no doubt of the reading. The substituted words, interlined by D, were deleted by C. 123 *clement,*] M, T print a comma only, but there seems clearly to be a point after it. 125 The writing avoids a small hole in the paper. 127 *flanders*] the *r* is malformed. 130 *ftraingers,*] T's comma is better than M's point, but the mark may be accidental. 131 *barbarous*] second *r* altered from *b* (not from *k* as T suggests). 136 *elamente*] T adds a comma but the mark is in the paper only. 137 *their*] M, T *ther* but there is little doubt of the reading. 140 *all*] belongs properly to the next line where T prints it. *momtanifh*] T *mountanish* noting '*un* only three minims': the writer's intention is quite obscure. *inhumanyty*] so M: T adds a point but it appears to be no more than a flick of the tail of *y* 141 *vs*] M and T both describe the deletion as being in modern ink, but on re-examination I am unable to distinguish it from that of other deletions and therefore ascribe it to C. The writer probably intended *lett vs* but forgot to cross out the *s*

~~eH~~ Linco

weele be ruld by you mafter moor yf youle ftand our
freind to ꝑcure our ꝑdon

moor

Submyt you to theife noble gentlemen
entreate their mediation to the kinge
gyve vp yor fealf to forme obay the maieftrate
and thers no doubt, but mercy may be found   yf you fo feek [yt]

---

147 *found*] *un* has three minims only.   *you*] *ou* malformed.   *yt*] M *it*: T omits.
D certainly wrote something after *seek* and the addition seems to me to improve the sense. The visible traces can be read *yt* (hardly *it*), but at the same time they are rather widely separated from the preceding word, and it is possible that they represent an & or some other sign indicating that the original text was to resume at this point.

FINAL NOTE ON CERTAIN READINGS IN Ll. 103–14.

103 *bis* (deleted)] The curious symbol superimposed on this word has certainly not the form of the & usual in English hands. It may, however, I think, be a loose attempt at rendering the print form of ampersand, which though rare is not unknown in manuscripts of the period. Since the ink in which the symbol is written is identical with that of the original writing, it seems unlikely that a second hand is involved in the alteration. This also applies to the contraction mark of *matie* in l. 101.

110 *and your*] T notes: 'a word was underlined for insertion between these two words, but it appears to have been wiped out while the ink was still wet. The traces of the letters seem to suggest *bend*.' It appears that *and* was crossed out and the word, whatever it was, interlined to replace it. But the whole alteration, which was probably never completed, has been erased. The traces are very illegible, but to me they suggest the letters *bye* rather than *bend*.

113 *warrs*] T *warre* noting that the writer 'altered *warre* to *warrs* by interlining a long *s*.' I am not myself able to detect any indication of a final *e*, and believe the supposed *ſ* to be the upward curl of the regular English final *s*.

112–4. In these difficult lines, if the original writer intended the interlined words *in in to yo͞r obedienc·* as a substitute for the two half-lines *why euen...by obedienc* (as has been suggested) one would have expected him to delete the latter. But, with the substitution of *hurly* for *warrs* he left the passage as it was, and must, I think, have meant it to stand. I conjecture that a stop was intended after *feet* in l. 111, and that *in in to yo͞r obedienc·* should be inserted between *ryot;* and *why*. The whole passage is clumsy but I no longer think, as I was once inclined to do, that the author was conscious of having left it in confusion.

For EU product safety concerns, contact us at Calle de José Abascal, 56–1°,
28003 Madrid, Spain or eugpsr@cambridge.org.

www.ingramcontent.com/pod-product-compliance
Ingram Content Group UK Ltd.
Pitfield, Milton Keynes, MK11 3LW, UK
UKHW010342140625
459647UK00010B/761